networking for development

Paul Starkey

IFRTD
The International Forum for Rural Transport and Development

Networking for development
©Paul Starkey
ISBN 1 85339 430 0

International Forum for Rural Transport and Development
New Premier House (2nd Floor)
150 Southampton Row
London WC1B 5AL
United Kingdom
Tel: + 44-171-278-3670
Fax: + 44-171-436-6880
E-mail: ifrtd@gn.apc.org
Webpage: http://www.gn.apc.org/ifrtd

Citation of this publication
Starkey P, 1997. Networking for development. International Forum for Rural Transport and Development, London, UK. 104pp. ISBN 1 85339 430 0

Design and composition: Krishan Jayatunge
Printed by: Biddles Ltd, Woodbridge Park Estate, Woodbridge Road, Guildford, Surrey GU1 1DA.

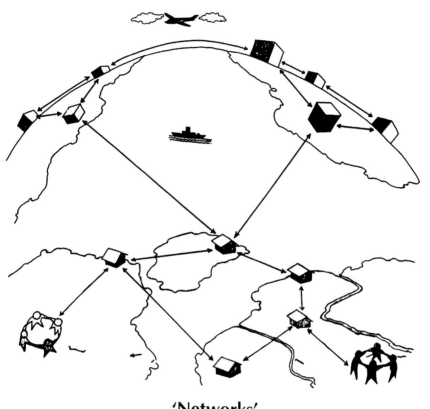

'Networks'

CONTENTS

Foreword 7

Preface and acknowledgements 9

Acronyms and abbreviations 11

PART 1: NETWORKS AND NETWORKING 13

Network types and networking benefits 14
Definition 14
Networking 14
The need for networks 14
Network typology 15
Electronic networks 17
Benefits of networks 20

General problems faced by networks 21
Lack of clear objectives 21
Membership disparity 21
Domination 23
Centralization and bureaucracy 24
Separate realities 25
Lack of resources 26
Manipulation of resources 26
Misinformation in networks 27
Competition 28
Donor interference 28
Monitoring and evaluation 29
Political constraints 30

General guidelines for networks 31
Objectives 31
Concrete activities 31
Committed core groups 33
Avoiding centralization through delegation 35
Decentralization of institution-based networks 35
Sharing, belonging and openness 36
Resources 38
Self-funding possibilities and problems 39
Legitimacy 40
Complementarity and linkages 42
Monitoring and evaluation 44
Network management 44
Beneficiary involvement 44
Network participation and benefits 46

PART 2: ANIMAL TRACTION NETWORKS IN AFRICA

PART 2: ANIMAL TRACTION NETWORKS IN AFRICA   47

The animal traction networks: experiences   48
Animal traction and the special need for a
    networking approach   48
Early animal traction networking initiatives   49
The West Africa Animal Traction Network:
    WAATN   50
Animal Traction Network for Eastern and Southern
    Africa: ATNESA   56

Lessons from the African networks   63
Open, independent, multidisciplinary networks   63
Working through workshops   64
Methodology of large workshops   65
Small thematic workshops   68
Coordination by steering committees   69
Communication channels   74
Seeing the benefits   75
Resources   76
Legitimacy and public awareness   81
Influence on policies   82
Raising professional standards   83
Training needs   84
Newsletters and information sources   85
Linkages with other networks   86
Farmer involvement   87
Monitoring and evaluation   89
Other practical problems   90
Conclusions   93

Appendices:
1) Further reading   95
2) Network contacts   100

FOREWORD

The International Forum for Rural Transport and Development (IFRTD) aims to be a *global network* of people and organizations promoting a broad approach to meeting the transport needs of rural women and men in developing countries. Lack of affordable transport inhibits agricultural productivity and economic activity. It isolates large numbers of people from health, education and other services. Rural women and men spend much time and energy on basic transport tasks. IFTRD advocates improving village transport infrastructure (tracks, paths, footbridges), establishing rural transport services and promoting intermediate means of transport to fill the gap between walking/carrying and large-scale motorized transport. IFRTD encourages an integrated approach to rural transport planning. This considers interventions that increase mobility and those that bring services closer to the community.

IFRTD was initiated in 1992 by people from several (north-based) development agencies. They formed an Advisory Committee and shared Secretariat duties between two member organizations. They initially concentrated on promoting the concept of the Forum and its innovative approach to rural transport. A mailing list of 800 persons and organizations world-wide was established, and a newsletter produced. National Forum Groups (national networks) were formed in Kenya and the Philippines and their representatives joined the Advisory Committee. At this stage there were no Forum activities and no framework for 'networking' among members. The Forum was largely synonymous with the information service of its Secretariat.

In 1995, the Advisory Committee decided a full-time Secretariat was needed to stimulate active networking. The Secretariat would liaise with national networks and promote interactions between them. It would encourage members to initiate National Forum Groups, with clear objectives and work programmes. The Secretariat now comprises three staff members and is hosted by the Intermediate Technology Development Group (ITDG). It publishes *Forum News* (in English, French and Spanish) and has a web page on the Internet.

networking for
development

7

By 1997, IFRTD members had formed National Forum Groups in Bangladesh, Burkina Faso, Kenya, The Philippines, Sri Lanka, Uganda and Zimbabwe. These are represented on the IFRTD Advisory Committee. Each local network involves people from many organizations and disciplines and acts as a pressure group for rural transport. In Kenya and Sri Lanka, Forum Groups have successfully lobbied for the inclusion of rural transport in national development plans and transport strategies. Network activities range from research to practical projects. Members in Tanzania, Uganda and Kenya are collaborating with the Kenya Network on Draught Animal Technology (KENDAT) to study how intermediate transport (including animal power) can improve the productivity of farming families. UK Forum members have set up an international e-mail discussion list. In Bangladesh and Sri Lanka the national networks are registered as a non-governmental organization and a non-profit company respectively. Other Forum Groups are considering formal establishment, while some are happy to operate on a less formal basis, delegating responsibility for network activities to different members.

IFRTD's mailing list now exceeds 1,000 people. The Secretariat has been stimulating network members to share their experiences, for example through the compilation of an annotated bibliography on rural transport and the preparation of case studies on gender issues. IFRTD members and Forum Groups are increasingly benefiting from active networking nationally, regionally and internationally. However, the Forum has yet to achieve the status of a global network. Members realise there will be much work and many difficulties to resolve as the Forum becomes more active and attracts more members and resources.

The ideas expressed by Professor Paul Starkey in *Networking for Development* have been an inspiration for the IFRTD internationally, and for the formation of active National Forum Groups. It is hoped that the valuable lessons contained in this volume will assist all Forum members, as well as others who use networking to achieve developmental goals.

Priyanthi Fernando
IFRTD Executive Secretary
London, December 1997

PREFACE
AND ACKNOWLEDGEMENTS

This publication derives from a network discussion paper (Starkey, 1992) prepared for the Animal Traction Network for Eastern and Southern Africa (ATNESA) and the West Africa Animal Traction Network (WAATN). That paper followed the author's participation in a workshop on Networking for Low External Input and Sustainable Agriculture held in the Philippines in 1992. At this workshop, 40 network facilitators and coordinators from around the world shared their experiences and discussed ways in which networks could be made more effective. The workshop was arranged by the Information Centre for Low External Input and Sustainable Agriculture (ILEIA), based in The Netherlands. It was hosted by the International Institute of Rural Reconstruction (IIRR), with support from World Neighbors.

The analysis of networks and networking presented in Part 1 derives from the experiences of the African animal traction networks as well as the papers, case histories and discussions of the ILEIA workshop. The workshop planning paper of Moelinono and Fisher (1992) which reviewed experiences of several networks in Southeast Asia was particularly helpful. Further information concerning the many network examples and workshop discussions may be obtained from the proceedings (Alders, Haverkort and van Veldhuizen, 1993) and a related volume prepared by Nelson and Farrington (1994).

Part 2 starts by explaining how the African animal traction networks developed and goes on to discuss some of the lessons learned. Presenting network experiences in this way has involved some inevitable selectivity and oversimplification. The animal traction networks are not offered as models, but as concrete examples of issues, achievements and problems that illustrate the general networking points summarized in Part 1. Further information on these networks can be obtained from the publications and network contacts listed at the end of this book.

The author would like to acknowledge and thank wholeheartedly all the people who made this publication possible. Firstly, the importance of the many members of the national and international networks is recognized. The

networking for development

author started preparing this work for his colleagues in the animal traction networks of Africa and Latin America. However, it soon became apparent that the lessons would be interesting to a much wider audience of diverse networks, including the national transport groups affiliated to the International Forum for Rural Transport and Development (IFRTD). This work is dedicated to all networks concerned with development issues.

Appreciation and acknowledgement goes to the organizers and hosts of the Philippines workshop (ILEIA, IIRR and World Neighbors). Gratitude is also due to GTZ (Deutsche Gesellschaft für Technische Zusammenarbeit GmbH, Germany) and Manfred Guntz for support to the animal traction networks in Africa and sponsorship of the earlier discussion paper.

Larry Fisher of World Neighbors and Eddie B Handono of Studio Driya Media, Indonesia, are thanked for allowing the thought-provoking Handono cartoons to enhance this document. The German Appropriate Technology Exchange (GATE) is acknowledged for the donkey technology cartoon on page 27. Much appreciation is due to Krishan Jayatunge for the book and cover designs and the desktop publishing.

Special thanks go to IFRTD and Priyanthi Fernando for arranging the preparation of this volume. Swiss Development Cooperation kindly contributed the publication costs. Particular appreciation is due to Dr John Twigg of the Oxford Centre for Disaster Studies who edited the text and provided some additional case history material.

This IFRTD book is also available in other languages. A Spanish edition has been prepared in collaboration with the Red Latinoamericana de Tracción Animal (RELATA). The Food and Agriculture Organization of the United Nations (FAO) supported the preparation of a French edition. The help of RELATA and FAO in allowing this work to reach a wider network audience is gratefully acknowledged.

networking for
development

Professor Paul Starkey
Reading 1997

ACRONYMS AND ABBREVIATIONS

AFSRE   Association for Farming Systems Research and Extension (global network)

AGROTEC   Agricultural Operations Technology for Small Holders in East and Southern Africa, Zimbabwe

APNEZ   Animal Power Network for Zimbabwe

AT   animal traction

ATNESA   Animal Traction Network for Eastern and Southern Africa, Harare

ATNET   Animal Traction Network Tanzania (subsequently TADAP)

BASIN   Building Advisory Services and Information Network

CTA   Technical Centre for Agriculture and Rural Cooperation, The Netherlands

DAP   draft (or draught) animal power

DAT   draft (or draught) animal technology

DGIS   Directorate General for International Cooperation, Ministry of Foreign Affairs, The Netherlands

ENAT   Ethiopian Network for Animal Traction, Addis Ababa

FAO   Food and Agricultural Organization of the United Nations, Rome

FOMENTA   Programa Regional de Fomento de la Tracción Animal, Managua

GATE   German Appropriate Technology Exchange, GTZ, Germany

GTZ   Deutsche Gesellschaft für Technische Zusammenarbeit GmbH, Germany

IDRC   International Development Research Centre, Canada

IFOAM   International Federation of Organic Agriculture Movements, Germany

IFRTD   International Forum for Rural Transport and Development, London

IIRR   International Institute of Rural Reconstruction, The Philippines

ILCA   International Livestock Centre for Africa, Ethiopia

ILEIA   Information Centre for Low External Input and Sustainable Agriculture, The Netherlands

networking for development

IMAG-DLO	Instituut voor Mechanisatie, Arbeid en Gebouwen (Institute of Agricultural Engineering), Wageningen
IRED	Innovations et Réseaux pour le Développement, Switzerland
KENDAT	Kenya Network on Draught Animal Technology, Nairobi
MandE	Monitoring and Evaluation (network)
MARTI	Ministry of Agriculture, Research and Training Institute, Tanzania
NAMA	Network for Agricultural Mechanization in Africa
NGO	non-governmental organization
PROPTA	Projet pour la Promotion de la Traction Animale, Togo
RELATA	Red Latinoamericana de Tracción Animal, Nicaragua
RESPAO	Réseau d'Etude des Systèmes de Production en Afrique de l'Ouest (WAFSRN in English)
RGTA	Réseau Guinéen sur la Traction Animale, Guinea
ROATA	Réseau Ouest Africain sur la Traction Animale (WAATN in English)
SACCAR	Southern African Centre for Cooperation in Agricultural Research
SAFGRAD	Semi-Arid Food Grain Research and Development Programme of the Organization of African Unity
SANAT	South African Network of Animal Traction, Fort Hare
TADAP	Tanzania Association for Draught Animal Power, Morogoro
UK	United Kingdom (of Great Britain and Northern Ireland)
WAATN	West Africa Animal Traction Network
WAFSRN	West Africa Farming Systems Research Network

networking for development

PART 1

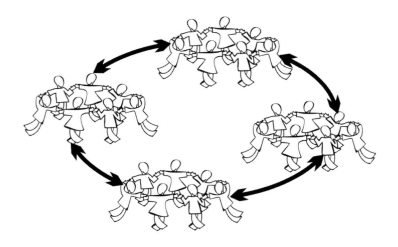

NETWORKS
AND NETWORKING

NETWORK TYPES
AND NETWORKING BENEFITS

Definition

A network is any group of individuals or organizations who, on a voluntary basis, exchange information or undertake joint activities and who organize themselves in such a way that their individual autonomy remains intact.

In this definition, important points are that the relationship must be voluntary, that there are mutual or reciprocal activities (i.e. exchange of information or joint action) and that belonging to the network does not affect the autonomy and independence of the members.

Networking

From the noun *network* are derived the verb *to network* and the participle *networking*. Networking involves making contacts and encouraging reciprocal information exchange and voluntary collaboration. In the view of the author, networking should encourage and facilitate the autonomy of colleagues rather than reinforcing dependency associations.

It will be argued in this book that the verb is more important than the noun: the process of networking is vital, and more crucial than a network structure.

The definition of a network given here makes it clear that not all information exchange or collaborative action can be described as networking. Dissemination of information, for example by television, radio, professional journals, abstracting services, newspapers and newsletters, is not, by itself, networking. Instruments of mass communication can be used by networks (many networks have newsletters) but they cannot be the sole basis for networks. Networks are not simply mailing lists, for they are based on mutuality and multi-directional information exchange.

The need for networks

In an ideal world, development networks would not be necessary, for individuals and organizations would be well linked vertically and horizontally with colleagues involved in similar areas (such as research, development, training, extension and infrastructural support). They would be in touch with reality, policy implications, new research initiatives and experiences in other places. They would be aware of the many technological, socioeconomic and administrative options available for Third World development, and their various advantages and disadvantages. They would have the resources to undertake their work, and would be able to collaborate with colleagues whenever this would be beneficial. Governments, organizations and communities would listen to them when they had recommendations to make.

Clearly such an ideal world is very far away! In reality, the many agents of development live in very separate worlds. Whatever their aspirations, they are effectively isolated from the wider experiences of others by the day-to-day problems of survival, repetitive work tasks and local interaction. This is so whether they be in the field or in the office of a non-government organization (NGO), international research centre, government ministry or aid agency headquarters. Information flows in government and non-government development organizations tend to be top-down and narrow, restricted to single disciplines, limited geographical areas and the prevailing organizational persuasion.

As a result, when a development 'wheel' appears to be required, the individuals or organizations use whatever is immediately to hand, and if necessary redesign or completely re-invent it. They seldom have the time, vision, experience or facilities to consider whether a 'wheel' is actually needed, what 'wheel' options are available worldwide and how these could be obtained locally in the available time (for 'wheel' read any relevant input, technology, training scheme, research idea, project proposal or other source of concern).

Networks can help overcome such problems by allowing people and organizations to exchange information and experiences with those outside their immediate working environment and cooperate with them in a legitimate and non-threatening way.

Network typology

There are many types of network and some people have tried to classify them by their membership, their geographical scope, their main activities, their objectives

networking for
development

15

and their organizational structure. All such classifications have some merit, but the diversity of networks is such that no system of classification is entirely satisfactory.

Illustrations of some of the network types discussed here are given in the diagrams on pages 18 and 19.

Membership criteria

Networks may be designed for, and restricted to, particular categories of people, such as farmers, researchers or engineers. Some bring together people working at the same 'level' (horizontal orientation, e.g. farmer-based networks), while others link those of different 'levels' (vertical orientation, e.g. those bringing together farmers, researchers, policy makers and international agencies). Some networks have individual membership, while others bring together institutions or NGOs. Some are open to all people and organizations interested in the subject covered by the network.

Geographical scope

Some national networks are limited to one area of a single country, while others are nationwide. Some international networks are limited to geographical regions (such as West Africa and Eastern and Southern Africa) or agroecological zones (such as the Arid Lands Information Network), while others are global in scope.

Network objectives

Most networks have been established mainly to improve information exchange among members, and information sharing is a primary objective. Some have been established to allow collaboration in research, education, training or marketing. Some networks aim to exchange materials (e.g. seeds for planting or prototype implements). Others exist to be pressure groups, to raise public awareness of issues and influence national or international policies in their area of interest. Many networks have multiple objectives, combining information exchange among members with practical collaboration in training and research and some public relations attributes.

networking for
development

16

Network management

Some networks are formal and highly centralized, with most communications passing through a strong, central secretariat. Others are informal and decentralized, and emphasize direct communication between members. Informal networks generally arose as 'grass roots' or 'bottom-up' organizations that have been formed as a result of user need. They have a tendency to aspire to, and sometimes evolve into, more centralized networks.

Misuse of the term 'network'

Some formal, centralized 'networks' which have arisen as a result of top-down planning by the international research centres, aid agencies or NGOs that fund them are not true networks based on the active participation and interaction of autonomous members. Some single-institution outreach programmes have, in reality, been dissemination units for information (in the worst cases, propaganda), technology or materials. Some have provided the parent institution with multi-country research or technology evaluation facilities, through a series of bilateral relationships that did not attempt to link the various clients. They have employed the term 'network' for public relations purposes. This is an abuse of the network concept that should be strongly discouraged.

Electronic networks

The development and spread of electronic mail has allowed people to participate in e-mail discussion groups and electronic workshops. Simple list-server software allows an e-mail message sent by one person to be relayed to all members of an agreed discussion group. People have the option of replying in front of the whole group (allowing public discussion) or may respond directly (allowing bilateral dialogue).

E-mail discussion groups have many network characteristics. People of different backgrounds working in a wide range of countries voluntarily join such groups. They share information and interact with other people of similar interests. Discussions can be spontaneous, or they can be moderated. Specific electronic workshops can be held over periods of weeks or months, to analyse issues in depth. Members of electronic networks and discussion groups may arrange other activities and face-to-face discussions from time to time, or they may simply interact electronically.

networking for development

17

Some network models

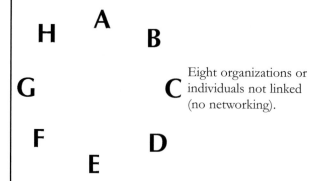

Eight organizations or individuals not linked (no networking).

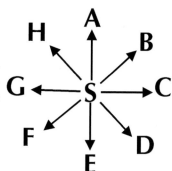

Information dissemination service from a central secretariat reaching the eight organizations or individuals, but no reciprocal information exchange (not a network).

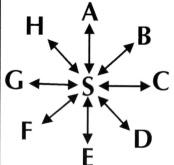

The organizations or individuals cooperating in a highly centralized network or institutional outreach programme. All have reciprocal relationships with the secretariat, but they do not network with the others.

networking for development

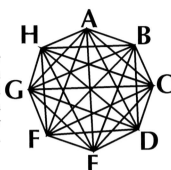

All the organizations or individuals linked with each other, without any central facilitation (theoretically a perfect network, but probably unrealistic).

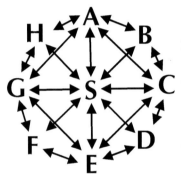

Network model with secretariat. The network members interact with each other (not all possible lines shown) and with a central secretariat that facilitates linkages between members.

Decentralized network model. Active national networks interact with each other and with resource organizations (not all possible lines shown). Secretariat responsibilities delegated.

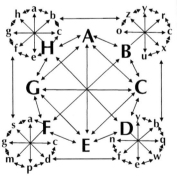

networking for development

19

Benefits of networks

Depending on their specific objectives, membership and activities, networks orientated towards development provide benefits in several interrelated ways. Some immediate and rapid benefits of the network are likely to be reflected in the work of the network members. Longer-term benefits become apparent as development and research programmes become more effective, know-how is transferred and systems evolve.

- Networks facilitate the exchange of information, skills, knowledge, experiences, materials and media, through meetings, workshops, publications and cooperative programmes. Sharing of skills and experiences increases the overall competence of network members, whether individuals or organizations.

- Network information exchange and coordination leads to less duplication of work and effort. With less duplication, faster progress and a wider overall impact should be possible.

- Networks can effectively link people of different levels, disciplines, organizations and backgrounds who would not otherwise have an opportunity to interact. For example, they can bring together top policy makers and farmers, agricultural engineers and animal scientists, NGO development workers and staff of large-scale technical cooperation projects, researchers and extension staff, university professors and village blacksmiths.

- Networks can create from separated people and organizations an awareness that many others have similar concerns and developmental problems.

- Networks can provide the critical mass needed for local, national or international advocacy, action and policy change.

- Networks can help address complex development problems and issues that seem overwhelming to those working at village level.

- Networks can bring together funding and technical cooperation agencies and those in need of resources and support.

- Networks can provide members with a source of peer support, encouragement, motivation and professional recognition. This can be particularly important to those outside the normal hierarchies of government, education and international research.

GENERAL PROBLEMS
FACED BY NETWORKS

Networks can face many organizational problems. Some of these are major structural and financial issues, while others relate to more subtle networking matters, such as the effects of the personalities involved. Some of these problems are discussed in the following sections (but the order in which they are presented here does not necessarily reflect their relative importance).

A valuable review of problems faced by networks was prepared by Moelinono and Fisher (1992): their findings were based on research in Southeast Asia but have a much wider application to networks in general. As part of their project, a series of cartoons was used to stimulate problem-solving discussions within the networks. Some of the cartoons, which were commissioned by World Neighbors, have been reproduced here.

Lack of clear objectives

Networks generally develop from clear needs identified by a group of individuals or organizations and so they have a vision and specific objectives. However, Moelinono and Fisher (1992) found that some networks had never clearly defined their goals. Without a clear purpose and specific objectives, they found it difficult to develop dynamic programmes with distinct targets that could be met. The networks became vulnerable to manipulation in the interests of dominant individuals or organizations. Network monitoring and evaluation became almost impossible, member interest was difficult to maintain, and such networks had little measurable impact.

'Lack of clear objectives'

Membership disparity

Networks with a wide range of members may experience difficulties in obtaining a balance of member involvement. Moelinono and Fisher (1992) described this problem as

Conflicts of interest

In Sri Lanka, an attempt was made to establish a network of NGOs and grassroots people's organizations to facilitate the exchange of information, expertise and resources. It was also intended that the institutional capacities of organizations taking part would be strengthened, which would ultimately lead to the empowerment of the poor.

The scheme was supported by Innovations et Réseaux pour le Développement (IRED), an international NGO committed to participatory development. IRED created a national resource centre in Sri Lanka to collect and share information and field experience among the network's members. The centre, around which the network was to be built, was managed by representatives of people's organizations and NGOs.

Soon after the network started, it broke down. It appeared that the NGOs and people's organizations had very different ideas about how the research centre should function and what resources it should contain. The NGOs were mainly interested in macro-level and policy issues, the people's organizations in specific operational matters such as how to run income-generating projects and registration procedures for NGOs.

It had been expected that the partners would treat each other on an equal basis and interact horizontally rather than vertically, but in practice the stronger NGOs were mainly interested in their own institutional survival rather than their partners' interests; and they also dominated decision making, maintaining a majority on the coordinating committee.

IRED therefore adopted a different strategy based on empowering people's organizations by setting up their own network to develop solidarity and reduce their dependence on outside agencies.

The story of this initiative illustrates several general problems facing networks: lack of clear objectives, the dangers of domination and membership disparity.

networking for
development

being one of hierarchical differences. Large, resource-rich agencies and institutions with well-educated, self-confident staff tend to dominate smaller organizations. The clear, coherent advocacy of the internationally-orientated staff may appear convincing in network meetings and this may unduly influence network programmes, even though members who are closer to grass-roots reality believe the approach or technology of the 'international' staff is inappropriate. Language can be a barrier to participation, with only those fluent in the official language (perhaps an external international language such as English) being able to contribute effectively.

'Hierarchical differences (membership disparity)'

A range of ideas and ideologies can be healthy for a network and stimulate creative tension and lively debate. However when strong-minded (and/or loud-mouthed) people with conflicting ideas meet, they can disrupt network meetings and progress with excessive ideological, methodological or technological debate. This can lead to alienation and withdrawal from the network by those who feel unjustly treated, or are simply bored.

Domination

Networks can easily become dominated by particular organizations, interest groups, political persuasions, ethnic groups, academic disciplines or other divisive influences.

'Domination'

Networks are often initiated by a few individuals or a single organization, who (whatever the formal status of the network) want only like-minded, compliant members. Membership and network activities tend to become limited to those favoured by the dominant group, using rigid criteria and narrow definitions. Jealousies and rivalries between individuals, disciplines or organizations can lead to the effective isolation of particular individuals or groups.

networking for development

23

Once the domination process has started, it is difficult to stop it, as membership, organizational responsibilities and the network agenda become controlled by one group. Individuals or organizations that feel dominated or excluded have little scope to change the network, and their attitude may become dismissive, disruptive or positively antagonistic. Unable to change matters, they may even initiate or join an alternative ('rival') network.

Electronic networks can easily be dominated by a few individuals. Some people dominate discussion groups by reacting to all incoming messages, while others 'chatter' to each other in a friendly yet exclusive way. An open, wide-ranging, international discussion group can quickly become dominated by a few people with very specific interests and limited geographical scope.

Centralization and bureaucracy

Centralization occurs when a network coordinator, secretariat, steering committee or board starts to control and run the network for its own sake, rather than coordinating and facilitating the activities of its members. This is often associated with network domination involving the secretariat, host organization or steering committee. Decision making is centralized and network communications are expected to pass through the central secretariat. Independently organized network activities are considered as unofficial or are even discouraged.

'Centralization' Many networks that start informally tend towards centralization. On the other hand, networks established by resource organizations and international institutes generally start centralized. Some of these try hard to devolve their responsibilities and activities to create a genuine participatory network. Others never break from the psychology of centralization, and the network centres tend to preside over passive or puppet networks.

Centralization is often associated with bureaucracy, where the secretariat, coordinator or steering committee become increasingly concerned with maintaining an office, handling correspondence and circulating a newsletter. Networking activities between members decrease and active membership falls. Outside observers may be unaware of the chronic problem, as the network offices appear active and the mailing list seems healthy (and may even grow as a result of passive membership).

The dangers of centralization are often only apparent when the network coordinator, secretariat and/or steering committee becomes inactive for a while (this might be due to work overload, sickness, resignation, lack of funds or attention to other duties). The network as a whole may simply cease to function. It may even die, because no one else feels they have the authority to convene meetings or restart activities.

Separate realities

In centralized networks, the secretariat or network coordinator is often based in a resource-rich institution and/or in a major city. While modern technology and comforts can make communications effective, they may also make the coordination unit increasingly remote from the realities of network members. While the elite are accustomed to efficient telecommunications and rapid inter-continental exchanges of e-mail, many people in the field still rely on frustratingly slow postal services.

Similarly, people participating in network activities may also be living and working in separate realities from those of the people they are supposed to represent. This is particularly true of certain officials of governments, NGOs and aid agencies who appear to spend a high proportion of their time attending workshops. Networks suffer because such people are not in close contact with the real actors in development, whom they claim to represent.

'Separate realities'

networking for development

Only people with easy access to computers and e-mail can join electronic discussion groups. Although e-mail technology is spreading rapidly, its users are still mainly people in privileged organizations, and e-mail groups tend to be rather elitist. Nevertheless, e-mail can be quite a levelling technology. Once connected, a young worker in a small rural NGO has the same access to the electronic discussions as a university professor or the director of a large government department.

Lack of resources

Networks often suffer from lack of funds for their activities and coordination. While members are generally prepared to sacrifice their time on behalf of the network, they seldom have sufficient funds for significant cash outlay.

In national networks, members may find it too expensive to travel to the capital city for a meeting or to visit colleagues working in remote rural areas. In international networks, the cost of airfares is almost invariably prohibitive for individuals. This means that unless the network has a specific budget for assisting travel, only resource-rich individuals or organizations can regularly participate in activities.

In some cases, members find even the price of international postage or telecommunications a significant personal burden. This fact is not always appreciated by their more fortunate colleagues in resource-rich organizations.

If networks do not have an adequate budget, they have to apply to resource-rich agencies to fund their activities. This has the possible advantage of the network having to justify its every action, but the bureaucratic process takes up much time and energy that could be better spent on actual networking.

Manipulation of resources

Where networks do have funds, for example as block grants, considerable tensions can be generated through the way the funds are administered. However democratically and fairly the money is dispersed, there may be jealousies and complaints. Both dedicated network members and mere opportunists will request funds for field trips, international travel and programme funding. Requests coming from the centre of the network (the coordinator, secretariat and steering committee) will tend to have first priority in resource allocation. These will probably be followed by nearby, influential colleagues and by those network members with whom good communications are easy (generally members living in towns and/or working in well-equipped institutions). The potential for genuine misunderstanding may be at least as great as that for intentional manipulation.

'Manipulation of resources'

Misinformation in networks

While networks can disseminate valuable information, some of the information being shared may be of dubious reliability, and some may even be false. For example, in the recent past, claims made in the field of animal traction for some animal species, harnessing systems and 'appropriate technology' contraptions have been so over-optimistic as to be potentially prejudicial to the unguarded reader. As a result, people have been encouraged to spend time and money on technologies that have already been shown to have little application.

Unless there is an atmosphere of questioning and self-criticism, inaccurate information can be spread among peer groups during national or international workshops. It is difficult for network members and coordinators to differentiate between accurate and inaccurate reports (whether verbal or written), particularly if they come from well-meaning network members.

'Misinformation..?'

Professional journals use academic referees and peer review to maintain standards. Such time-consuming processes are unlikely to be acceptable to people compiling simple newsletters. Questioning the conclusions or validity of a report can be seen as offensive to some, and might easily be construed as unreasonable criticism, attempted censorship or a form of network imperialism. The very openness of network experience exchange makes it easy for 'misinformation' to be spread. The only antidotes are likely to be friendly, constructive criticism, a willingness to admit mistakes and close attention to actual experiences.

networking for development

Competition

Networks can be affected by competition from other networks or organizations with overlapping agendas. This can lead to creative collaboration, but it can also lead to competition for recognition, limited resources and membership. Donor agencies can use the existence of an alternative network as an excuse not to fund the activities of an apparently similar network.

In some countries there are quite small numbers of influential people that development networks may wish to involve and influence (e.g. deans of technical universities, heads of government departments). Network multiplication and fragmentation make it impossible for such people to participate in all network meetings, and so the networks become susceptible to the whims of favouritism.

'Competition'

Resource-rich organizations that are unhappy with a particular network (perhaps due to professional differences, jealousies or the network's resistance to domination) may be able to use sponsorship to lure members to alternative events or workshops. Busy professionals have only limited time available for networking, and competition is likely to damage disproportionately those networks that are low-profile and resource-poor.

Donor interference

Donors or resource-rich institutions may use their financial muscle to influence network policy. This may be expressed through biases in work programmes, skewed participation in meetings and a form of censorship of network publications.

networking for
development

28

Network members tend to be intimidated by donor and resource institution representatives. Network core groups seldom argue with such people, being concerned not only for network funding but also for any possibilities of external assistance to their own careers and programmes. Although the parent institutions do not officially condone interference in autonomous networks, some resource organization representatives are known to enjoy being in a position of power, and exploit its potential for effective manipulation.

In extreme cases, a single donor can effectively close down a centralized network by cutting off its funding. The influence of individual funders and resource organizations can be greatly reduced through multi-donor sponsorship of networks and their activities.

Monitoring and evaluation

There seems to be relatively little experience relating to the monitoring and evaluation of networks. This is partly because, by their very nature, networks tend to be informal and loose structures that wish to emphasize future progress and not past experiences. Active, dynamic networks are too busy networking and achieving to devote limited time and resources to introspection; torpid or inefficient networks do not wish to risk being exposed to criticism. Even informal self-evaluation procedures require searching self-examination and criticism. This could be uncomfortable, even in highly successful networks, and it could be quite traumatic in low-achieving organizations.

'Monitoring and evaluation ...'

Farmer request

Some centrally-established networks have tried to undertake evaluation exercises: they include the Arid Lands Information Network established by Oxfam and the networks of the Overseas Development Institute. These evaluations have involved membership surveys, reviews of existing information and evidence of changes, peer group reviews and records of publications and citations. Some research networks funded by the International Development Research Centre (IDRC) have undertaken participatory internal evaluations (and monitoring) and external analyses of constraints and programmes.

Network ideas

Even highly centralized and structured networks have found it difficult to define reliable indicators of network success and to quantify the effects and the benefits of networking.

Final solution?

Numbers can be given for certain outputs such as network members, newsletters (number of issues, pages, recipients), letters answered, meetings arranged (participant numbers, participants' backgrounds, topics covered), network proceedings and publications, visits arranged, etc.

networking for development

However, such quantitative figures give no indication of quality: 100 active members may be better than 1,000 names on a mailing list; one in-depth workshop or network publication may be of more value to members than two superficial ones (or, conversely, two simple workshops or publications may be more useful than one detailed one).

Numbers may give a general idea of a network's activity level, but they not do give a fair impression of its effectiveness.

To make evaluation even more difficult, there are the 'iceberg' and 'snowball' effects (which have more relevance to tropical networks than their names suggest!).

• With active, devolved networks, the activities that can be easily quantified by the central group are but the visible tip of an iceberg, with many more actions and benefits occurring unseen.

• One small idea learned at a network event can cause individuals and programmes to change their whole work emphasis or methodology, and improve their effectiveness immeasurably. Similarly, a brief workshop encounter can lead to a whole series of 'snowballing' follow-up, secondary contacts and collaboration, which, although the direct result of network actions, are not necessarily known about by the network leaders.

Political constraints

National and international networks have to operate within the political realities of a country or region, and unstable or repressive regimes are not uncommon. In some countries, information exchange is viewed with suspicion, and government clearance is required for all correspondence, newsletter contributions, field trips and workshop attendance.

Intolerance of criticism is also common, making it difficult for networks to advocate alternative policies towards development (for example relating to economic or mechanization policies, grass-roots associations and credit).

GENERAL GUIDELINES FOR NETWORKS

Although the catalogue of potential problems presented above may seem large, most networks are able to overcome many or all of the constraints. Most networks are able to work effectively.

Nevertheless, some clear lessons emerge from the analysis of problems. These are presented in the following pages in the form of generalizations and guidelines. They are intended to stimulate further interest in the issues of effective network operation, not as a comprehensive guide to network structure and function.

Objectives

Networks need to establish clear objectives, which will determine their direction, their core activities, and the types of individual and organization likely to be active members. The objectives should be formulated with a wide cross-section of members (to prevent domination).

Network objectives should be periodically reviewed, in order to assess progress made towards meeting them and their continued relevance.

Networks should be prepared to evolve with time and to change their objectives as circumstances change and their initial goals are met. Networks may be temporary arrangements to tackle particular needs and when these are achieved the networks may have to transform themselves radically to tackle new objectives, or even dissolve themselves.

Concrete activities

Networks need to initiate concrete activities that are interesting and beneficial to members. The driving force of a network can be maintained through enthusiastic participation at specific activities that allow member interaction and sharing.

Superficial activities lead to superficial networks. Active networks cannot be maintained only by the circulation of newsletters. Lengthy mailing lists are no substitute for

networking for development

31

Turning committment into outputs

Duryog Nivaran is a network founded in November 1994 to reduce the impact of natural disasters and conflict in the South Asian region, principally by influencing other agencies through research projects and advocacy activities such as workshops.

Much of its project work to date has been undertaken by steering committee members and a few other founder members, who are NGO staff and independent researchers. Although other agencies and individuals are now being drawn into new projects, and links are being developed with other networks and organizations in the region, this has been a slow-moving process. Communications across the network have also been poor, a problem which can only partly be explained by technical problems with post, telephone, fax and e-mail.

Duryog Nivaran has therefore depended largely on the small number of its core members for its outputs. All of these members are enthusiastic about the network's aims but at the same time they are heavily involved in other work and have not been able to give as much time to network initiatives as originally hoped. As a result, the network's projected outputs of books and seminars have been much delayed, causing concern at the agency that hosts the network's secretariat, which is responsible for reporting on progress to Duryog Nivaran's main donor.

To its credit, the network has been prepared to discuss these matters openly at its steering committee meetings and in front of donor representatives. It is now drawing up new long-term plans in the light of experience, which will be more realistic about what outputs are feasible. There is also a clear need to expand the active membership, in order to reduce dependence on the current core group. Another option the network might consider is replacing some of the busier steering committee members with people who can devote more time to the network.

networking for
development

face-to-face discussion and the experience of working closely with network colleagues to solve common problems.

Concrete activities do not have to be arranged by a central group. Network members can arrange activities themselves. These may be open to the whole network or to specific groups of collaborators (e.g. geographic or thematic sub-groups). In an active network, there will be a wide range of activities taking place, some arranged by the core group but many more arranged by a variety of network members.

Electronic networks also need concrete activities if they are to maintain people's interest and sense of belonging. These need not involve face-to-face discussions, but they have to have clear purpose and outputs. E-mail discussion groups can arrange electronic conferences on specific themes, resulting in guidelines or proceedings (which might be published in book form to benefit non-members).

Committed core groups

Although wide participation is most important, networks need a committed core of active members who will take initiatives and be responsible for coordination, management and logistics. The individuals or organizations in this core group must be prepared to look beyond the immediate bounds of their own organization and their day-to-day activities, and give network affairs that most valuable of commodities: time.

Since almost all individuals and organizations involved in development feel pressured by excessive demands on their time and resources, network business will only receive adequate attention if it is considered a priority. The people (or organizations) volunteering for, or assigned to, a network core group should consider the success of the network as an explicit objective of their professional lives and work. The global impact of some social movements (e.g. ecology, women's rights and democratization) has been largely due to highly effective networking organizations run by small groups of committed volunteers.

The core group must be, and remain, representative of the network's members. It must interact regularly with a variety of ordinary members to keep up with their ideas and changing needs. Without such interaction, network core groups tend towards centralization and increasing isolation.

networking for development

33

Delegation

The Association for Farming Systems Research and Extension (AFSRE) has no full-time staff. Its office holders are elected to specific executive positions and the network board for one or two years.

Initially most board members came from universities in the USA; more recently, they have come from a variety of universities and organizations around the world. Their organizations have generally provided administrative support during their period of elected responsibilities. There has been no single secretariat but different board members have been responsible for overall network representation, membership lists and fees, workshop organization, the network journal, networking liaison and nominations for future elections.

Centralization and institutional domination have been largely avoided through this system of voluntary work, by people who regard the honour and professional contacts of the position as sufficient compensation for the time-consuming nature of the allotted tasks.

To further the process of decentralization, the AFSRE board members for the different continents have been encouraged to establish autonomous but inter-linked regional associations to organize information exchange and workshops at a regional level. The major AFSRE workshops now rotate between the regions.

networking for development

There has to be a continual process of renewal within the leadership group, through rotation of responsibilities within the network and by democratic election and selection.

The core group should regularly, and self-critically, review not only its progress but also its own relevance to other network members. To help networks maintain a realistic approach, clearly orientated towards their ultimate beneficiaries, creative ways of including beneficiaries or their representatives in network management systems should be considered.

Avoiding centralization through delegation

The network, and its core group, should make a point of delegating network responsibilities to a variety of individuals and organizations. This will help avoid the dangers of excessive centralization, domination, isolation and passive membership. Some networks have avoided centralization by delegating specific coordination responsibilities to different members of the steering committee (see the case study of the Association for Farming Systems Research and Extension above).

Network members should not expect all network activities to be arranged by the core group. Members should feel themselves responsible for arranging or assisting in appropriate network activities. If a network appears inactive, members should blame themselves as much as any core group.

Electronic networks can delegate the task of stimulating discussion or moderating debate over specific periods to different people. Members can be asked to raise issues for future debate, and the task of preparing background information and/or introducing the topics can be delegated to different individuals.

Decentralization of institution-based networks

Donor-established information-sharing networks and international research networks have generally started with a central secretariat and full-time staff. These tend to be fairly formal networks, with international donor

Decentralization: from institution to network

The Building Advisory Services and Information Network (BASIN) was established in 1989 to disseminate advice and information on appropriate building technologies for use in the Third World.

Its principal activity is an integrated technical inquiry service where each member agency handles information on a particular area of building (such as roofs or walls); this has been supplemented by publications, research projects and seminars. Although BASIN describes itself as a network, for its first six years it had only four members, all European agencies, who had founded it; and it was not open for others to join. It can be regarded more as an institution-based service for disseminating information than a network proper.

An external evaluation of BASIN in 1996 showed that the technical inquiry service and information materials were of high quality, but the outreach should be greatly extended in order to meet the considerable need in the Third World for expert advice on building technologies.

The evaluation suggested that this could best be achieved by involving Third-World agencies more fully as partners in providing and disseminating technical information, and would require the four European core members to spend more time assisting local partners to undertake activities. In other words, what was required was decentralization, a wider and active membership, and information exchange rather than one-way dissemination. Through such a process, BASIN would become a more authentic network.

In fact, BASIN had already begun to recognize the need to move in this direction. It had begun to widen its membership by recruiting a fifth member agency, from Kenya, and it is now planning ways of taking the process further in the light of the evaluation's recommendations.

networking for
development

36

involvement and a prestigious host institution. The institutional base may enhance international recognition and facilitate funding, but it should not stop the delegation and decentralization of network activities.

If institution-based networks are to avoid being mere information dissemination services and/or outreach departments their central units should help to facilitate independently organized activities by network members. This will not only enhance the members' professional experience, status and responsibilities but also improve prospects for network sustainability in the event of the central unit closing down.

Several donor-created international networks have attempted to stimulate greater membership participation by devolution. For example, some have developed decentralized units concentrating on the needs of particular geographical areas or ecological zones.

Sharing, belonging and openness

A sense of participation and inclusiveness is vital to network success. Decision-making processes, the choice of network activities and their means of implementation should be democratic, and allow members to feel they can influence events. Networks should welcome participation from a broad range of individuals and agencies concerned with their objectives. Networks can provide a relatively informal, non-threatening framework for exchange, discussion, debate and cooperation between institutions and individuals. This encourages the sharing and synergy that is fundamental to network success.

There are bound to be certain conflicts of interest between members. These may include competition for limited network resources, workshop locations, training facilities and representation on steering committees, or the advocacy of competing methodologies or technologies. To ensure network harmony, and to prevent exclusion and fragmentation, these issues must be seen to be tackled and resolved in an open and clearly fair way.

networking for development

37

Resources

Networks do need resources to be effective. Funding is not everything. This is illustrated by the low impact of some resource-rich networks established by international institutions. By contrast, some networks without any central funding have achieved a remarkable impact, due to the willingness of their members to dedicate their time, effort and personal resources to network activities. Nevertheless, money is required for international network participation, and the combination of member enthusiasm, involvement and *adequate* funding seems ideal.

A network needs to anticipate and plan for the funds it requires to implement activities, and it needs a recognized structure to secure and manage such funding. A guiding principle should be to keep overhead and operational costs to a minimum. Obtaining and managing funds generally requires much time and energy from network members, who may not be experienced in this. To maintain network credibility (to members and to sponsors) funding should somehow be managed or supervised by a broad coalition of members.

Members and agencies that contribute towards a network are likely to be committed to its success. The more a network can be user-supported, the stronger it will be. User-supplied resources do not have to be financial. One research-development network has made it a point that although membership in developing countries is free, all members *must* regularly contribute 'in kind' through written articles and professional feedback.

Networks can benefit from being associated with a sympathetic local and/or international agency that can provide access to resources, additional contacts and institutional support services. However, safeguards may be required to prevent such institutional arrangements leading to centralization and/or domination. A network that depends on a single institution or funding agency is highly vulnerable to domination, and even to the sudden termination of its resources at the whim of that agency.

Networks are likely to require external sponsorship for expenses relating to international travel. This is particularly true for networks when they operate in countries with currencies that are not readily exchangeable. Networks can minimize the need for expensive air flights by emphasizing national-level networking events and arranging international meetings at locations that allow some, or all, participants to take cheaper, surface transport. To maximize the benefits of international travel, those taking part in international networking activities should also be actively involved in national networking events.

Self-funding possibilities and problems

Most networks are funded directly or indirectly by one or more aid agency or benefactor. However, there are some that are financially independent (for an example, see the case study of the International Federation of Organic Agriculture Movements above).

In the more developed countries, some networks such as professional or disciplinary associations can generally fund many, or even all, of their activities through a combination of subscriptions and voluntary work. Their individual members are relatively affluent (compared with the less developed countries) and so can afford subscriptions and a reasonable level of travel and communications expenditure from their own pockets. Moreover, they often work in organizations such as universities that are favourably disposed to the network or association, and accept a reasonable amount of networking activity within official work time. Through their places of work, members and network officials are often able to benefit (officially or unofficially) from efficient support services, low-cost photocopying and easy telecommunications.

Access by network members in the South to efficient communication facilities is much more difficult. Finding photocopiers and working telephones can be a problem

networking for development

even in government departments and universities. Staff of resource-rich development projects may have access to good administrative support, but such projects are generally geared to the rapid achievement of short-term goals and their staff are seldom allowed to devote much professional time to organizing network activities.

Some national-level professional associations in Asia have been able to fund their own activities from a combination of subscriptions, voluntary work and supportive host institutions. This is much more difficult for international networks. Due to low salary levels, foreign exchange problems and high bank charges, the payment and collection of international network subscriptions is seldom practical.

The Association for Farming Systems Research and Extension (described on page 34) is a professional association with a world-wide scope but no full-time staff which has benefited from much voluntary work and university support. It has endeavoured to meet many of its running costs from membership dues which have been collected mainly from members based in the North and those attending international symposia. Nevertheless, its international mailing, major networking events and travel sponsorship have only been possible through grants given by aid agencies.

Legitimacy

A network and its leadership need the support and trust of their own members. They also benefit from wider legitimacy within the social and political environment in which the network operates. Legitimacy attracts participation and facilitates funding. It does not necessarily imply conformity, but networks that are collaborative and inclusive are generally more effective than those that are confrontational and exclusive.

Legitimacy can be enhanced by involving well-respected people at networking events and well-targeted publicity. Legitimacy and recognition can be assisted by the repeated use of an easily identifiable name (or acronym) and network logo.

The long-term reputation of a network may be affected by the quality of the information, experiences or technologies

Achieving legitimacy

The Shelter Forum is a Kenyan network which aims, through collective action, to make affordable and decent housing more widely accessible to vulnerable groups in society. Its activities encompass advocacy, networking, extension, institutional strengthening and research.

The legitimacy and credibility achieved by the Forum have been demonstrated by its considerable influence on the official revision of building by-laws and regulations. It was also invited to sit on a national steering committee drafting a national plan of action to be presented at the United Nations Habitat II conference on shelter in Istanbul in 1996, and took an active part in that conference. Contacts with agencies in other countries are increasing.

A number of reasons may be presented for the Forum's success in gaining legitimacy and influence. One, of course, is the fact that it addresses an issue of considerable concern to policy makers and planners.

A second reason is the range of its members, both by number and type. It seeks to bring together 'key players' and currently has a membership of some 800 stakeholders of different kinds (community-based organizations, NGOs, local authorities, government ministries and the private sector), who debate issues and share information. To lobby effectively for policies that favour marginalized groups, the Forum has relied on well researched information, which an extensive dialogue with these different stakeholders can provide.

Other reasons include the Forum's clear commitment to giving practical support to poor rural and urban communities and those who work with them. It seeks to disseminate practical information on low-cost shelter delivery mechanisms and technologies as widely as possible through the existing media. Its active extension programme provides specialized advice and support to members who are at a disadvantage because of lack of capacity, experience or resources.

networking for
development

being promoted or exchanged. Network core groups, workshop facilitators and the editors of publications should endeavour to ensure that any information disseminated is legitimate. This should not justify attempts at academic or intellectual imperialism. Research and development networks are likely to benefit from core groups that have technical expertise, a sympathetic but questioningly-critical approach and a close understanding of grass-roots reality.

Complementarity and linkages

There is scope for different networks tackling similar issues in different ways. Such networks will have their own 'niches' which can be, and should be, complementary.

Geographical scope is one clear basis for complementarity: different networks can operate at local, national, regional and global levels. Other complementary 'horizontal' networks may be based on different organization type (NGOs, farmers, research institutions, etc.) or disciplines (animal science, agricultural engineering, rural sociology, transport, etc.). Such networks can have different (but overlapping) objectives, programmes, membership and management systems, reflecting their particular scope and target audience.

There is also an important need for 'vertical' networks that help to bring together the views and experiences of beneficiaries, extension agents, researchers, policy makers, aid agencies, financiers and the private sector.

Inter-network links are necessary to:

* enhance information exchange between different groups

* encourage constructive collaboration

* avoid competition

* reduce duplication of services

* improve the targeting of network benefits

* allow maximum benefits to be drawn from the different comparative advantages of beneficiaries' groups, national networks and international resource organizations

Formal or informal linkages should be established and actively maintained through joint activities and mutual representation at relevant workshops and coordination

Electronic networking and its potential

Electronic networking is on the increase but this is still a relatively new area, with many lessons to be learned and experiences to be shared.

One of these new electronic initiatives is called MandE (which stands for Monitoring and Evaluation). It aims to provide a means for disseminating information on innovations in monitoring and evaluation practice, primarily among NGOs but also bilateral and multilateral agencies. Membership is free and open to anyone with an interest in the subject. MandE describes itself as a 'managed market' concerned with the exchange of information, rather than as a network; but many who use it refer to it informally as a network.

The electronic form was chosen because it is cheap and convenient. In particular, it makes it possible to spread news about innovations rapidly, to share a large amount of material over a very wide geographical area, and to be highly responsive to demand for particular types of information. On a home page on the WorldWide Web, MandE presents short news items submitted by members; this material is also distributed by e-mail to members who do not have access to the WorldWide Web.

The network aims to keep management and editorial control to a minimum, in order to encourage the maximum participation and exchange of information. At the moment, the system is relatively centralized and formal, with the Web site and e-mail list managed from a single point and a word limit for news items circulated.

However, the idea is that members seeking more information about a particular innovation in monitoring and evaluation will be able to obtain this from the originators. In the longer term, this could well lead to much broader networking among the members independently of the centre. Perhaps this trend will stimulate evolutionary change in the structure and goals of MandE, but at the time of writing the network was less than a year old, making it too early to see how it may develop.

networking for development

43

meetings. If overlapping networks coexist without linkages, their members or core groups should ask searching questions about the true nature of their networks, and the implications of such lack of cooperation for their members and target groups.

Monitoring and evaluation

Networks, like all organizations, require regular and thorough monitoring and evaluation. Not only should work plans be continually assessed relative to network objectives, but network progress and achievements should also be periodically evaluated. For many reasons discussed previously, the monitoring and evaluation of networks is extremely difficult. Despite, or because of this, the very process of attempting to assess the effectiveness of network activities is likely to be educational for all involved.

Network management

Network management is complicated, and few people have had training in this field. The success of many networks demonstrates that much can be achieved by groups of enthusiastic amateurs without professional training in management. However, it should not be necessary for all networks to have to learn entirely from their own experiences and mistakes. Regionally-based training courses relating to networks could be beneficial.

Beneficiary involvement

Networks orientated towards improving sustainable development need to make an effort to encourage beneficiary participation in networking processes. For example, agricultural research and development networks would be more likely to achieve their aims if they developed appropriate ways of ensuring that farmers' views and experiences were considered or represented in all the relevant aspects of their networking.

networking for
development

44

National and international networks are likely to gain from close association with area-specific or national beneficiary-based networks. Exchanges between beneficiary groups in different parts of a country, and between countries, could

Beneficiary involvement

The most active people in many development networks are professionals from NGOs, international agencies, research institutions and the like. These are not, of course, the ultimate beneficiaries, who are different groups of poor and marginalized people. The need to involve the ultimate beneficiaries or end-users in networks is generally recognized, but this can be hard to achieve in practice.

The attempt is more likely to succeed if the beneficiaries are genuine participants in network dialogue and information exchange. Moreover, a lot of grass-roots networking takes place horizontally and informally, not through formal channels or network structures. Formal networks, and other institutions, are well advised to work with such mechanisms, and there is much to be learned from them.

A good illustration comes from Nicaragua during the 1980s, when government agricultural policy aimed to empower peasant farmers (*campesinos*). There was a shift in emphasis from top-down information dissemination by NGOs to informal farmer-to-farmer exchanges (the *Campesino* to *Campesino* Movement) in which NGOs and the main networking forum, the national farmers' union, took on more of a facilitating role.

The movement was based upon farmer-promoters who were willing to experiment with alternative techniques and share their experiences with others. Commonly, these would work with NGOs to give workshops to others within or outside their own communities. The NGOs supported the process by providing technical assistance or finance for training and field visits.

After the success of initial trial schemes, news of the movement spread rapidly throughout the country. This was done in a spontaneous fashion, through informal channels of communication between the *campesinos* themselves. Soon, *campesinos* in nearly every part of Nicaragua were coming to NGOs and their national union calling for assistance in launching similar initiatives. The process was being driven by networking from below, not above.

networking for
development

45

be particularly valuable. Network members can help establish contacts between local groups and facilitate follow-up actions.

Network participation and benefits

Ultimately, participation in any network will be determined by the perceived benefits that individuals and organizations see in it. Members need to have a stake in the general objective, an interest in specific activities, a desire to contribute, a sense of belonging, respect for the network, trust in its leaders and a confident feeling of achievement and future possibilities.

If network objectives are appropriate and inter-institutional linkages are in place, active, decentralized programmes of beneficiary-orientated network activities should make a significant contribution to sustainable development.

networking for development

PART 2

ANIMAL TRACTION
NETWORKS IN AFRICA

networking for
development

THE ANIMAL TRACTION NETWORKS: EXPERIENCES

The first part of this book discussed general lessons concerning networks and networking. This section is a detailed case study focusing on the experiences of two regional African animal traction networks and their associated national networks. These experiences illustrate many of the general issues discussed in Part 1.

Animal traction and the special need for a networking approach

The employment of domestic animals for tillage or transport is known as animal traction. Cattle, buffaloes, donkeys, mules, horses, camels and other working animals can provide smallholder farmers and transporters with vital power for crop cultivation, transport, raising water, milling, logging, levelling land and road construction.

There are many regions of the world where animal traction has been used for thousands of years. It remains an important aspect of rural life and culture. This is true of many parts of Asia, the Middle East, North Africa, Ethiopia and Southern Europe. There are other parts of the world, notably the Americas and South Africa, where animal traction has been used for centuries, rather than millennia. In some other areas animal traction has been adopted this century. This is true of most of sub-Saharan Africa and also areas of transitional farming and new settlement in Asia, the Caribbean and Latin America. In some locations animal traction is being introduced at the present time, and the process of introduction will carry on into the next century.

In North Africa, the Nile valley and the Horn of Africa, there is a long history of using animal traction for soil tillage and transport. Elsewhere in sub-Saharan Africa, animals have long been employed for transport by certain pastoralists and traders. However, in most African countries, the use of animal traction in smallholder farming systems was introduced in the twentieth century. In many cases the technology, usually involving pairs of work oxen and imported metal implements, has been pioneered during the lifetime of the present elders.

networking for
development

48

During the 1960s and early 1970s animal traction received relatively little attention from newly independent governments. This was a period when many people thought that the rapid tractorization recently seen in Europe and North America would take place in African countries.

However, by the late 1970s higher oil prices, foreign exchange shortages and numerous failed tractor schemes suggested that rapid motorization was not, after all, practicable. Animal traction started to be seen in many countries as a serious, but neglected, development option.

With the inflow of donor funds that followed the well-publicized Sahelian droughts, many donor-assisted projects were established in Africa to introduce or expand the use of animal traction technologies. These projects tended to work in isolation, unaware of each other.

Early animal traction networking initiatives

In 1982, the Food and Agricultural Organization of the United Nations (FAO) convened an expert consultation on animal traction which concluded that improved information exchange was extremely important. As a follow-up, FAO organized missions to 12 African countries to investigate the possibilities of establishing an animal traction network. These were implemented in conjunction with the International Livestock Centre for Africa (ILCA) based in Addis Ababa.

The missions found that there was very little information exchange between animal traction programmes within countries, let alone between countries. There were far too many cases of projects, a short distance from each other, 're-inventing the wheel' (or redesigning an implement) in almost total isolation.

The missions concluded that a network was not only extremely desirable, it was also very feasible. There was strong support for the idea both at the level of projects and institutions, and also in national ministries. It was suggested that it might be most practicable if a network were to be launched in West Africa, to be quickly followed by complementary initiatives in Southern and Eastern Africa.

networking for development

49

The West Africa Animal Traction Network: WAATN

Although the FAO/ILCA proposals had stimulated interest in the creation of a network, there was no immediate follow-up. However, in 1985 the Farming Systems Support Project of the University of Florida arranged a regional workshop in Togo to discuss animal traction in the context of crop-livestock integration. This 'networkshop' was probably the first time that people from several anglophone and francophone countries in West Africa had come together specifically to discuss animal traction technology and review it from a farming systems perspective.

The 30 participants regarded the event as extremely useful, and resolved to hold a follow-up workshop which would allow further in-depth analysis of the issues and enable more countries in West Africa to exchange information. They launched the West Africa Animal Traction Network (WAATN) by electing a steering committee that was charged with arranging a larger, follow-up workshop. The steering committee comprised representatives from animal traction programmes in five West African countries together with a representative of the main resource organization (the University of Florida) and a facilitating technical adviser (the author of this book). The steering committee met later in 1985 and recommended several activities designed to improve information exchange between countries and with other networks. Emphasis was placed on workshops, exchange visits and publications.

Workshops

In 1986, a workshop on 'Animal power in farming systems' was hosted by the national animal traction programme in Sierra Leone. It was attended by 73 people from 20 countries, and the published proceedings contained 34 papers. This was followed, in 1988, by a workshop on 'Animal traction for agricultural development', hosted in Senegal by the national agricultural research institute. The WAATN steering committee then asked network members from Nigeria to organize a workshop, and in 1990, the workshop on 'Research for development of animal traction' was held in Kano.

networking for
development

These workshops, organized every two years in different countries, were the main, visible activities of the West

Africa network. In its first five years, WAATN workshops were attended by over 200 people and every West African country was involved. The workshops stimulated the preparation and publication of 150 papers covering a wide variety of issues and experiences concerning animal traction in different farming systems and related research, development, extension, training, implement production and policy implications. The workshops proved extremely popular, and the detailed evaluations conducted at the end of each one revealed that participants considered them interesting, helpful and professionally valuable.

WAATN publications

The West Africa Network published its workshop proceedings in collaboration with the German Appropriate Technology Exchange (GATE), ILCA and the Technical Centre for Agricultural and Rural Cooperation (CTA). These books were available free of charge to people working in Africa. Non-participants, seeing such attractive proceedings, were encouraged to put their own experiences in writing for subsequent workshops.

GATE also published an animal traction directory and an animal traction resource book based largely on the networking experiences and approach. ILCA published an animal traction bibliographic database, made possible by the same networking approach. These publications were also free of charge to network members in Africa.

Major improvements in information exchange between animal traction workers occurred in West Africa following the various workshops and publications. Most document exchange was on an individual-to-individual, or organization-to-organization basis. Thus documents produced in Mali, Sierra Leone, Togo and Senegal (for example) are now commonly found in other countries in the region. This was not the case when the network was launched. While there was no official West Africa animal traction newsletter, the Togo animal traction newsletter, *Force Animale*, was circulated to network members for several years.

networking for development

51

Other WAATN activities

The large workshops and their proceedings were the most obvious examples of the work of the West Africa network, but numerous other activities also took place. During the period 1985-93, the WAATN steering committee met once or twice a year. As these meetings included field visits, they also acted as group study tours. They increased committee members' experience and resulted in mutually beneficial interactions with the animal traction specialists of the host country.

Although formal network events have been important, the majority of WAATN's networking activities have been carried out by country programmes themselves, and by the members of particular interest groups. All members of the network have been free to communicate directly with other members. Thus, many visits, study tours and collaborative activities were arranged on a bilateral basis between different organizations in the region.

Programmes in West Africa have also collaborated with research and development organizations in Europe. Although visits and collaboration have been arranged directly between members of the network, they have often been stimulated by contacts made as a result of workshops or network publications. They can be considered under the network umbrella in that they involve collaboration between members. Moreover, the information produced has been reported during workshops and has also diffused informally through other networking contacts.

National networks in West Africa

Active national networking developed within several West African countries. In some this was achieved through projects or programmes operating at a national level. For example the Sierra Leone Work Oxen Programme helped to coordinate animal traction research and extension through a national committee and workshops, and national and provincial ploughing competitions. In Togo, networking was stimulated by the national coordinating project and its newsletter. In Nigeria, a network was launched during a WAATN meeting in 1990. In Guinea, a non-governmental organization, Réseau Guinéen sur la Traction Animale (RGTA), was created in 1992 specifically to facilitate national networking.

Elsewhere national networking has tended to be stimulated by donor-assisted projects operating in particular parts of a country. For example, technical manuals, discussion documents and videos produced through projects in countries such as Benin, Burkina Faso, Mali and Cameroon have been circulated widely within those countries.

Attempts to institutionalize WAATN

The informal WAATN management system of the early years was able to achieve results, but the steering committee did not consider it ideal. Lack of funds was felt to be a major constraint. The committee therefore made various proposals to institutionalize WAATN and fund it adequately. Ambitious project documents were prepared on two occasions. These had budgets large enough to hire and house a full-time network coordinator (a West African with an international salary), equip a secretariat and provide operating expenses.

The donors approached rejected the proposals as being too expensive. One point raised was that the animal traction network had operated effectively for several years without a large budget. Thus it was difficult to justify major financial provision if the network seemed capable of working well without it. The relative success of enthusiastic volunteers and part-time amateurs had actually made it more difficult to obtain the services of full-time professionals.

Self-help

Attempts were made to try to combine the benefits of voluntary work with longer periods of committed time. One donor, the International Development Research Centre (IDRC), offered to provide funds that would allow committee members to take time off their main jobs, and work for a few months on specific network activities. This creative proposal was received by the steering committee with mixed enthusiasm. It was perceived by some as a distinctly second-best alternative to the requested full-time coordination rather than as an improvement to the existing system.

Collaboration

ILCA offered in 1988 to coordinate a formal animal traction research network from its headquarters in Addis Ababa, drawing on the informal West Africa Animal Traction Network. A steering committee would have had overall responsibilities for the network, but day-to-day coordination would have been undertaken (and paid for) by ILCA.

This offer was put to the general assembly of WAATN in 1988, but was politely declined, mainly because of fears of losing control of the network to one member institution. Members were under the impression that international research centres had, in the past, used networks to promote their own interests rather than those of the members. Furthermore, such centres had mandates limited to research, while the network wished to ensure that it continued to serve the needs of those more concerned with development, extension and implement production.

Association or domination?

Negotiations started concerning a formal association between WAATN and the West African Farming Research Network (WAFSRN) which had established an independent secretariat in Ougadougou under the umbrella of the Semi-Arid Food Grain Research and Development (SAFGRAD) programme of the Organization of African Unity. Draft protocols of understanding were drawn up with both WAFSRN and SAFGRAD, and it was envisaged that the animal traction network would continue to operate as a fully independent network, under SAFGRAD, sharing offices with WAFSRN.

In 1990, WAFSRN decided that if WAATN wished to share its facilities, it should become a sub-network. The WAATN steering committee did not want to become a subcommittee. It was worried that the network might be swallowed up.

ILCA then offered to host the network secretariat at its offices in Kaduna in Nigeria, promising independence. The offer had definite attraction, although Kaduna had poor international communications and there was still some concern that the network would lose its autonomy, in practice.

In 1991, both WAFSRN and ILCA assisted with some travel costs for WAATN committee members, and the steering committee tried to negotiate suitable terms for collaboration. No final decision was taken, partly because none of the planned committee meetings resulted in a quorum. The situations of the possible host institutions altered significantly in 1991-92: the WAFSRN network coordinator resigned and two key ILCA animal traction personnel moved. The WAATN steering committee, which had started to rely on ILCA and WAFSRN to instigate planning meetings, was not convened in the first half of 1992. The momentum for establishing a coordination unit, and planning a programme of activities, had reached a low point.

Lack of formal programme

While much informal networking continued to take place in West Africa in the early 1990s, no formal network activities were arranged to follow-up the 1990 Nigeria workshop.

In an attempt to revitalize network coordination, the national animal traction network of Guinea, RGTA, invited the WAATN steering committee to attend a farmer-based workshop in Guinea in 1992. Both ILCA and WAFSRN made renewed offers of support and collaboration. The steering committee (which had changed little in composition since the start of the network) elected a new chairman. He was mandated to continue discussions with WAFSRN. ILCA offered to host the next meeting of the steering committee in Mali, where a new major workshop could be planned. The committee discussed possible thematic workshops, but did not mandate any particular organization (such as RGTA) to organize one on behalf of the network.

The steering committee expected to meet again within a few months to finalize institutional arrangements and a work programme. However, ILCA did not host another committee meeting as planned. The situation within WAFSRN also changed. The committee did not have the resources to meet again formally.

Thus, after more than eight years of negotiation, the West Africa Animal Traction Network was unable to achieve its desire for a full-time secretariat and network budget. Although discussions with donors and possible partner organizations have always been entirely harmonious, there remain unresolved conflicts of interests. The network will almost certainly have to lose some of its independence if it is to have a full-time coordinator and secretariat.

networking for development

With the clarity of hindsight, it appears that while the steering committee was repeatedly attempting to secure adequate funds and the institutional arrangements to operate the network effectively, it was unintentionally falling into the traps of centralization and isolation. Without a programme of activities or publications to benefit members, the network core group was appearing increasingly irrelevant to the many animal traction programmes in West Africa. At the field level, member enthusiasm, volunteerism and project-linked funds were still available, just as they had been at the launch of the network. Delegation had been lacking, and so formal network activities had ceased.

Informal networking continued in West Africa, and WAATN members participated in many animal traction activities organized by other networks. Between 1992 and 1997, several West Africans participated in workshops in Eastern and Southern Africa. They called for the West Africa network to be revived with new vision. Several initiatives have been proposed, and it remains to be seen whether or not the network will be formally relaunched.

Animal Traction Network for Eastern and Southern Africa: ATNESA

In 1987, the Southern African Centre for Cooperation in Agricultural Research (SACCAR) organized a regional animal traction workshop in Maputo, Mozambique. At this it was resolved that a regional information-sharing network should be established. Although SACCAR was unable to follow up the networking proposal, several individuals from Eastern and Southern Africa participated in workshops organized in 1988 (Senegal), 1989 (Indonesia) and 1990 (Scotland and Nigeria). On each occasion, the participants from the region met and affirmed that they should form their own animal traction network.

An opportunity to launch such a network came in November 1990. The setting was a regional course on planning integrated animal draft programmes, held at the Agricultural Engineering Training Centre of the Institute of Agricultural Engineering in Harare, Zimbabwe. During the course, the experiences of the West Africa Animal Traction

networking for development

56

Network were presented and there was much discussion about regional networking. The participants therefore selected six people from different countries to form a committee to discuss organizational details and prepare an action plan. The decisions of this committee to launch a network and organize a major workshop were endorsed by the final plenary session of the course.

The provisional steering committee of the new Animal Traction Network for Eastern and Southern Africa (ATNESA) met again in Zambia in 1991 to discuss network structure and to plan the first major workshop. The committee recommended an informal system of organization based on national networks linked through a regional steering committee. There were no immediate plans to establish a secretariat. The day-to-day management of network activities and workshops, and associated correspondence and fund-raising, was to be delegated to national networks and specific interest groups.

ATNESA held its first large, open workshop in Zambia in 1992. Over 100 people from 17 countries took part, and most were sponsored by their own organizations (or agencies within their own countries). The workshop was arranged by a multi-institutional committee, strongly supported by the Ministry of Agriculture and associated development projects. The core costs of workshop planning and implementation were provided by the Directorate General for International Cooperation (DGIS) of The Netherlands, in collaboration with the Dutch Institute of Agricultural Engineering (IMAG) that was supporting several Zambian animal traction programmes.

The workshop followed the pattern established by the West Africa network, with the emphasis on field visits and small group discussions. Where possible, invited lead papers were prepared collaboratively, with experts (or resource organizations) in two or more countries combining their experiences prior to the workshop. The workshop also provided opportunities for members with specialized interests to plan collaboration and coordinate activities. Among the special interest groups that met were people interested in farming systems research and extension, gender issues, local manufacture of implements, donkey power, cart design and animal-powered systems.

networking for development

During the workshop, two open general assembly meetings were convened. At the first meeting, organizational arrangements and draft statutes for the network were discussed and an *ad hoc* committee was nominated to finalize them. At the second meeting, the statutes were formally adopted. Some of the statutes were similar to those of the West Africa network, but greater emphasis was placed on the role of national networks. It was stated from the outset that the network would function largely through the interaction of autonomous national animal traction networks and direct contacts between the different programmes in the region. Limits were also placed on the time steering committee members could serve.

A new steering committee was elected, comprising representatives of six national networks (or animal traction programmes) and two people from interested resource organizations. The steering committee was given a mandate to arrange a programme of activities based on the workshop recommendations. However, the steering committee stressed that while it would help stimulate, coordinate and facilitate such a programme, the actual responsibility for implementing network activities would be that of individual ATNESA members in different countries (perhaps with support from resource organizations).

ATNESA's programme

In the light of the workshop discussions, the steering committee proposed the following networking activities, to be implemented by various network members.

- Establish formal or informal national animal traction networks in as many countries in the region as possible.

- Facilitate the holding of small international workshops on specific themes, such as gender issues, animal-powered transport, weed control, donkey use and conservation tillage.

- Collect and collate information on organizations and individuals involved in animal traction in the region for use in national and regional mailing lists. Such information could form the basis of an ATNESA directory of people and resources to assist organizations to recruit people from nearby countries as local consultants.

ATNESA workshops

The first wide-ranging ATNESA workshop was held in Lusaka, Zambia in 1992 on the theme of 'Improving animal traction technology'. It was attended by 107 people from 17 countries; over 80 technical papers were circulated. The 480-page volume of proceedings was published in cooperation with CTA.

The workshop on 'Gender issues in animal traction' was held in 1992 in Mbeya, Tanzania. This was attended by 32 people from Tanzania, Zambia and Zimbabwe. The participants reviewed project experiences and discussed ways in which women can gain more from animal traction technology. A booklet of guidelines was published as a result.

'The design, testing and production of animal-drawn carts' was the subject of a workshop held in 1993 in Harare, Zimbabwe. As a result, a 190-page resource book of guidelines was published in collaboration with IT Publications.

A workshop on 'Weed control using animal power' was held in 1993 in Tanga, Tanzania, attended by 64 people from 14 countries. Fifty technical papers were edited to form a resource book.

'Meeting the challenges of animal traction' was the theme of ATNESA's second wide-ranging workshop held in Karen, Kenya in 1995. The 130 participants came from 27 countries and 85 technical papers were edited for the proceedings.

The thematic workshop on 'Improving donkey utilization and management' was held in Ethiopia in 1997 and was attended by 85 participants from 23 countries. Two resource books are being prepared as outputs.

networking for development

- Increase awareness of the existence, aims and objectives of ATNESA through formal publications, publicity materials and contributions to newsletters and journals.

- Arrange major, wide-ranging workshops, with general assembly meetings, every two to three years.

The initial activities of ATNESA are shown in the box on page 59. Since the network has emphasized decentralized operations, not all ATNESA-stimulated activities can be listed. Many network-related activities involving international collaboration have been arranged by ATNESA members within the context of their national programmes or in conjunction with complementary networks (farming systems, agricultural engineering, transport forum, etc.)

ATNESA secretariat

In 1996, ATNESA was provided with the resources to establish a small secretariat in Zimbabwe, in conjunction with the Animal Power Network for Zimbabwe (APNEZ). The office (vacated by an international project) was well-equipped but did not have full-time professional staff. A specific ATNESA newsletter was not produced (not simply for reasons of time and resources, for it was recognized that other newsletters, such as *South African Network of Animal Traction Newsletter* and *Draught Animal News*, were already being circulated to ATNESA members). Thus the initial impact of the secretariat was quite small: ATNESA activities continued on a decentralized basis.

National networks in Eastern and Southern Africa

ATNESA aims to work largely by stimulating direct contacts between members in the region. It encourages the formation and interaction of national animal traction networks which are autonomous although they are affiliated to ATNESA (see box on page 61).

The national networks have similar goals, and seek to improve information exchange and collaboration through various means including meetings, workshops and printed materials. They generally aim to influence national policy in favour of animal traction, and are in better positions to lobby governments than an international network. They are also able to involve the local users of animal power (farmers, transporters, village blacksmiths) and a wide range of

networking for development

60

National networks in Eastern and Southern Africa

The Animal Power Network for Zimbabwe (APNEZ) was launched in 1994. Its voluntary secretariat has been based at the Institute of Agricultural Engineering. APNEZ has held several workshops, some arranged in collaboration with other organizations, such as Silsoe Research Institute.

The Ethiopian Network for Animal Traction (ENAT) was launched in 1994 at a two-day national workshop opened by the Minister of Agriculture and attended by 120 people. Following a period of inactivity (with internal discussions on its organization and status) it was relaunched during the ATNESA workshop on donkeys held in Ethiopia in 1997.

The Kenya Network on Draught Animal Technology (KENDAT) was formed in 1992. It was formally established as a national NGO. With help from a Dutch-supported project, KENDAT set up an office based at the University of Nairobi. It held national workshops in 1993 and 1995, and hosted the second major ATNESA workshop in 1995. It has published extension leaflets, publicity materials and workshop proceedings.

The South African Network of Animal Traction (SANAT) was formed in 1993. Its secretariat, based at the University of Fort Hare, publishes a twice-yearly newsletter. SANAT organized a nation-wide appraisal survey and published a book summarizing local animal traction issues. It has held both national and provincial workshops and training courses, and published proceedings. SANAT is due to host the third major ATNESA workshop.

The Tanzania Association for Draught Animal Power (TADAP) was launched in 1991 (initially as ATNET). It was formally established as an association with a Board of Trustees in 1996. Staff of the University of Morogoro, MARTI Uyole and the Ministry of Agriculture have assisted with coordination. It has held national workshops and published proceedings. It hosted the ATNESA regional workshop on 'Animal power for weed control' in 1993.

Zambia does not have a named network, but it has a strong national networking programme. This was developed by a specific Ministry of Agriculture animal traction coordination project and an associated research, development and training programme. These programmes hosted the first major ATNESA workshop. Nation-wide animal traction surveys and national workshops have been organized, and the results published. A twice-yearly newsletter, *Zambian Animal Draft Power*, has been widely circulated.

At a national workshop in 1995 it was agreed to start a Mozambique national network affiliated to ATNESA. Discussions on the establishment of national networks have also taken place in Botswana, Malawi, Namibia and Uganda.

individuals and organizations concerned with specific aspects of animal traction (manufacturers, transport ministries, animal welfare groups, credit agencies, donor representatives).

Representatives of the ATNESA steering committee and/or invited guests from neighbouring countries have attended workshops and activities organized by the national networks. This has reinforced linkages and strengthened mutual recognition and legitimacy.

ATNESA workshops

ATNESA regards occasional large (over 100 people), wide-ranging workshops as vital for general information exchange and the cross-fertilization of ideas. However, smaller workshops focused on specific themes are also needed to allow specialists to concentrate on particular issues. Smaller workshops for 30-60 people can be organized relatively simply and cheaply in cooperation with national networks or interested host organizations.

In addition to the main ATNESA workshops (see box on page 59), ATNESA has collaborated with other organizations and national networks, to tackle topics of mutual interest, such as implement design and on-farm research programmes.

LESSONS FROM THE AFRICAN NETWORKS

Open, independent, multidisciplinary networks

The international and national animal traction networks in Africa have achieved a great deal in the past 12 years. Many lessons can be learned that could benefit future networking initiatives. The networks are all African organizations that developed from informal contacts. They did not arise from project documents of donors, nor were they created by resource institutions. They have grown up from strong member interest and close collaboration with a variety of donor organizations.

The networks are open to all people and organizations sympathetic with their aims and objectives. Network members have come from a wide range of disciplines and organizations, so that the networks have not been dominated by any one discipline, job type or special-interest group. Researchers, planners, policy makers, extension workers, teaching staff, trainers, veterinarians and implement manufacturers are all active members.

Most members are salaried staff working in the public or NGO sectors (ministries, local, national or international development agencies, research institutions and educational establishments). Private sector people and organizations are also members, and these include implement manufacturers, consultants, farmers' unions and individual farmers. Most members are African nationals, but up to one third of participants at international workshops may be expatriate technical cooperation staff or representatives of non-African institutions.

The networks have had no intentional gender biases, but only about 10-30 per cent of network members and workshop participants have been women (to the regret of the network organizers). While the proportion of women participants has been increasing, men are still predominant in those projects and institutions that are working on animal traction in Africa.

While the ultimate aim of the networks has been to benefit the end-users of animal power (the smallholder farmers

networking for development

and transporters) most network activities have been designed to improve the work and effectiveness of network members. The networks have concentrated on information exchange and collaboration between members as the best means of achieving their objectives. This has led to publications, workshops and joint activities in training, research and development. Farmers and farmers' groups have been directly involved in the national networks. In the international networks, it has been assumed that farmers' interests have been represented by the individuals and organizations working with them (directly or indirectly; perfectly or imperfectly). Nevertheless, the views of farmers, transporters and artisans have been heard in all international workshops and planning meetings through farm-based discussions.

The networks have received support from several donors and international institutions, but they have not been dependent on, or controlled by, any single one of these. Such flexible structures have allowed the networks to survive despite major policy and financial changes among resource organizations. Also, the multi-donor support has prevented any one funding agency using its financial muscle to impose its particular policies and priorities on the networks.

The networks have achieved recognition and legitimacy primarily through effective programmes with clear outputs. They have been assisted by their easily recognizable logos and well-targeted publicity. Network continuity has been assisted by member enthusiasm, flexible communications channels and multi-donor support. Network members have been encouraged to correspond directly with their colleagues in other countries. This has reduced centralization and prevented communications bottlenecks developing.

Working through workshops

Large, open, multidisciplinary workshops and smaller thematic workshops, and the resulting resource documents, have been the most visible activities of the international and national networks. The workshops have been important for attracting new members and maintaining membership diversity (disciplines and functions). They have provided opportunities for network business meetings to discuss plans and elect new steering committee members. Without broadly-based workshops, the networks and committees could easily become dominated by one particular occupation, discipline, geographical area or language group.

The participatory and farmer-orientated workshop methodology employed has been a significant factor in the success of the workshops. Their openness and size have allowed new individuals and organizations in different fields and occupations to participate and keep the networks fresh. There have been many cases where open workshops have brought together colleagues who were working within the same country but were previously unknown to each other.

The workshop planning and implementation process has been assisted by the detailed evaluations carried out at every event. This has allowed the topics, programme and participatory techniques employed to evolve in the light of participant feedback.

Methodology of large workshops

Open invitations

The workshops have been well publicized in advance, with an open invitation to all those working in the field of animal traction. This is unlike the 'closed' international workshops more commonly organized in Africa, where attendance is only by specific invitation. Participants have had to meet certain conditions, such as the preparation and submission of a suitable paper or poster. When an excessive number of people from the same country have applied to attend a workshop, selections have been made based on the quality of these papers, and the need for a suitable balance of different organizations and disciplines.

As a result of the open invitations, the workshops have been thoroughly multidisciplinary with agricultural engineers, economists, animal scientists, agronomists, sociologists and other professions coming together. Furthermore, the participants have come from different professional fields, with researchers, extension workers, administrators, producers and donor representatives all interacting closely.

networking for
development

Local organization

The organization of the workshops has been the responsibility of local committees. The most effective ones have been those with highly committed core groups and broad membership (allowing inputs of human and logistical resources from many different local organizations). The local committees have been briefed on the good and bad points of past workshops, allowing each new committee to build on previous experiences.

A single hotel or training centre offering both accommodation and workshop rooms has been selected as the workshop venue. All participants (national and international) have been required to stay here, generating an excellent working atmosphere. Experience has shown it can be divisive if participants stay in different hotels, and it is disruptive and time-wasting if participants have to commute to a separate conference venue.

Workshop papers

Participants have received copies of all the papers prepared, most recently in the form of a workshop reader. However, they have not spent much time sitting through long sessions of paper presentations (which people tend to find tedious). Rather, there have been a few selected key papers, designed to stimulate discussion. Where possible, these key papers have been prepared by collaborating groups of national and international experts. Consideration has been given to the communication skills of the presenters, as well as their technical knowledge.

Stimulating networking

Informal discussion has been stimulated at an early stage in the workshops by 'networking announcements'. All participants have been able to summarize briefly their work and interests, and the topics on which they would like to exchange information during the week. Sometimes these have led to special evening sessions for those with particular interests, which have led in turn to subsequent collaboration. Some national and international networks have started as a result of such evening sessions. Provision of a participant address list at the start of the workshop has assisted networking interaction.

Information exchange has also been assisted by 'poster sessions' and exhibitions. Participants have been encouraged to prepare visual summaries of their work. These have included posters summarizing scientific research, photo exhibitions and displays of harnesses and equipment. They have been available for discussion during coffee breaks and evenings, as well as special poster sessions.

Field visits

Without doubt, the most popular elements of each workshop have been the field visits. People who have been to conferences where field visits involve large groups slowly straggling around research sites may be surprised at this. The popularity of the visits has been due to the detailed on-farm discussions held with farmers and their families. Small groups (five to eight people) from different countries have travelled to villages to talk with individual farmers (women and men) and, where possible, to watch work animals in use and artisans at work.

In-depth discussion with farmers is an integral part of participatory appraisal and farming systems research. However, it has often been a revealing experience for workshop participants. Even those familiar with such techniques have benefited from the focused discussions. Some visitors have felt free to ask farmers questions they would never dare to ask in their own countries, for fear that their juniors would laugh at them. The groups have also visited village blacksmiths.

The more intense and individual the nature of the discussions, the higher has been the value for participants. Thus if groups of visitors have been large (ten or more), or farmers have been brought together for a formal meeting, the opinion expressed in the evaluations has been somewhat less enthusiastic.

Groups returning from discussions with farmers have briefly visited project sites, research stations and implement producers. These additional visits have not only added interest to the day, they have also allowed participants to assess the relevance of such activities in the light of the morning's discussions.

Small group discussions

On the day following the field visits, the groups have sat down to discuss their observations and findings in detail. Following open discussion on the issues raised, new groups have been formed to discuss specific workshop themes and action plans.

Special interest groups have formed during the workshops and this has allowed the broad, inter-disciplinary farmer-centred discussions to be complemented by detailed analysis and planning by colleagues working in similar areas. The various small group discussions have proved almost as popular as the field visits.

Evaluation

Before they leave, participants have been asked to complete detailed evaluation forms, which have included plenty of scope for open-ended comments and ideas. The analyses of such forms have allowed the steering committees to plan future workshops concentrating on the most valuable aspects, trying to eliminate previous problems and unpopular elements.

All the workshops have stimulated networking interactions and contacts. Informal discussions and encounters have led to a wealth of subsequent information exchange and valuable practical collaboration between members. Many participants have stated in their evaluation forms that a major workshop benefit was 'meeting others working in the same field'.

Each workshop has resulted in hundreds of member-to-member exchanges. Most have been invisible to the steering committee and workshop organizers, although a few have been documented in letters of thanks that have included lines such as 'following the workshop we have started to work closely with ...'.

Small thematic workshops

Both international networks have advocated the holding of small workshops to tackle particular themes.

Unlike the broadly-based workshops, thematic workshops are intended to bring together people from particular ecological zones, occupational interests or disciplines. Thematic workshops can be relatively small (perhaps 20-25 people from three to six countries). This makes them relatively easy to fund and organize. In many cases overland travel is possible, reducing the expense and organizational problems associated with air flights. Costs can also be kept low by using rural training centres or inexpensive hotels (which is seldom practicable for major workshops that require many rooms).

Among the topics suggested in West Africa were animal power in rice-production systems, weeding and tillage, and the design and manufacture of implements. The West Africa network did not manage to arrange small workshops, but ATNESA has held workshops on several issues (gender, carts, weeding and donkeys).

In addition, several national networks have held their own small workshops, and have benefited from the networking approach by inviting participants from a few neighbouring countries. For example, participants from Zambia and South Africa were invited to a workshop on tillage systems held in Zimbabwe.

Some of the organizational and methodological lessons of the large workshops have applied to thematic workshops. Arrangements have been delegated to local organizing committees, which have been briefed on previous network experiences. Emphasis has been on participatory discussions rather than paper presentations. Farmer-centred field visits have proved popular. Participants have been invited to give feedback through evaluation forms.

From each workshop, resource publications and/or guidelines have been produced and circulated to other network members. This has spread the lessons learned, and given the donor agencies confidence that past, present and future sponsorship is justified.

Coordination by steering committees

All the animal traction networks have been controlled by steering committees (or boards). Some steering committees have proved very effective, in the short term, but have gradually declined in their ability to manage and delegate. Other steering committees have maintained their effectiveness. Some national and international networks have shown symptoms of centralization, with the core

networking for development

69

group becoming increasingly isolated and irrelevant to the animal traction programmes operating in that country or region.

There are clear lessons to be learned, but it is often difficult to differentiate between the operational system and the individuals involved. Certain people, strong or weak, can influence events for better or worse, whatever the management system. Moreover, some individuals work well together, while others do not; and this can be crucial for small committees meeting occasionally to plan network activities. Some people like the idea of being on a committee, but do nothing between meetings. Some national networks have held frequent, long meetings, so discouraging the involvement of busy people and those living far away.

Composition

Both international networks have had steering committees comprising six people from different African countries, plus two members of resource organizations (determined by the general assembly). The members have generally been nominated in their individual capacities, and have not been official representatives of their countries (some have been officially endorsed by their organizations after the elections).

In both constitutions, there have been clauses requiring the electorate to try to maintain a balance on the committee with respect to geographical zone, discipline, language and gender. A perfect balance has never been possible, but electoral officers have offered guidance during general assembly meetings. The electoral procedures have varied, but divisive elections have been rare and in many cases some or all committee members have been elected by acclamation.

The position of network technical adviser has been a voluntary appointment, determined by the steering committee, although in some cases the general assembly has recommended the continuation of the work of the incumbent (the present author).

The steering committee of WAATN was fairly constant for a period of ten years. At general assembly meetings, participants proposed that the existing committee members should be returned by acclamation. While this gave valuable continuity and stability, the limited turnover of committee members restricted opportunities for fresh vision and new dynamism. This became particularly noticeable after attempts to institutionalize and fund the network fell through. ATNESA has learnt from this and has adopted statutes that restrict steering committee members to a maximum of two terms.

Delegation

A small steering committee meeting occasionally can only operate effectively through delegation. Duties have to be delegated to various steering committee members, and to people and organizations outside the core group.

After its initial six years of effective activity, the West Africa network started to show signs of core group centralization. The lack of steering committee activity was quickly reflected in reduced formal networking in West Africa. The steering committee had not been able to implement an active programme itself. More importantly, it had not delegated the responsibility for organizing particular activities to other members who might be in a better position to do so.

The ATNESA steering committee has attempted to delegate specific tasks to individual members, and to follow up assignments. For example, the task of planning and implementing different workshops has been assigned to different national networks, with between one and three years lead time. Other delegated duties have included compilation of national and regional directories, compilation of existing extension material, secretariat duties, financial control and liaison with other networks.

To help maintain momentum, ATNESA has adopted a system whereby agreed actions, delegated duties and time limits for their achievement are clearly listed and circulated. Those accepting responsibilities are expected to check regularly on their own progress and report back to their colleagues. This helps all members give priority to their committee duties in the face of their routine work loads.

If steering committee members or other volunteers find they cannot cope with their assigned tasks they must reassign their duties to other colleagues or stand down. Traditional politeness can be disastrous for a network, and so colleagues should be willing to challenge inactive members and suggest they be active, delegate or resign. In this way, active network cores should be maintained, while the achievements and professionalism of the committees are also enhanced.

Structure or function?

One clear lesson that emerges is that network activities are more important than formal structures. At a regional level, WAATN and ATNESA have been very active and achieved much despite their informal structure and lack of formal secretariats. While many network members believe that strong, active coordination units would be highly desirable, the absence of these has not prevented the networks from flourishing.

The different national networks have opted for a range of management options: some are legally established, others associated with universities or ministries. Their relative success also appears to have been due more to member and core-group enthusiasm (and access to resources) than structures. Some national networks (including Zambia and Togo) have involved national projects that have not used the term 'network' in their titles, yet these have been able to stimulate national and international networking through their activities.

Network secretariats

National and international networks can operate without full-time secretariats, provided there is adequate division of the workload and clear delegation. In both WAATN and ATNESA, the host organization of a workshop has acted as a temporary secretariat for the planning and implementation of that activity.

Most national networks have individuals or organizations designated as secretariats, although these are run by network members acting in a voluntary capacity with their network duties peripheral to their main work. The KENDAT and SANAT national networks have offices and secretarial staff located within universities, but the networks only pay recurrent costs.

networking for development

The national and international networks could all benefit from good secretariats, provided that care is taken to avoid centralization. Given the expense of establishing fully independent offices, it might be best if secretariats were established in association-neutral institutions that would not dominate them. The steering committees would have to clearly define the roles of the secretariats and the particular attributes of the person(s) who were to be responsible.

The presence of a secretariat and the process of centralization are *not* the same. Nevertheless, once a secretariat has been established, there is a strong temptation to delegate all organizational responsibilities to it, rather than involving a variety of network members. An ineffective secretariat (like an ineffective steering committee) is worse than nothing, for active members feel unable to undertake duties already assigned to someone else. With this in mind, ATNESA has been making a conscious effort to develop its secretariat gradually, continuing to place greatest importance on activities developed by national networks.

Special assignments

Experience has shown that prior to (or instead of) full-time secretariats, much can be done through a combination of delegation, voluntary work and special assignments.

Steering committees can delegate specific duties to suitable network members who have the interest, ability, technological capacity and time to undertake them. For duties that require a longer period of concentrated work the steering committees can arrange 'special assignments', with assistance from a resource organization or donor agency. This has already been the case with some workshops and publications.

The system could well be developed further, so that different network members (not necessarily on the steering committee) would be assisted financially to undertake periods of full- or part-time work (a few days or weeks at a time) in order to arrange a network activity or prepare a publication. Such measures would not only strengthen network coordination, they would also assist the professional development of network members.

A creative system of this kind would depend on the regular interaction of committee members (they would be expected to meet at least twice a year, perhaps at thematic workshops). It would require rigorous self-monitoring of progress and achievements by the steering committees and critical evaluation by the general assembly meetings.

networking for development

73

Communication channels

By keeping the networks open and informal, communication channels have tended to be reliable and efficient. Naturally, respect has been given to national and institutional protocols, but within such limitations, network members have been encouraged to correspond directly with their colleagues in other countries. Such direct contact, combined with copying relevant correspondence to interested parties, has proved very effective.

Some members have argued that all communications should be channelled through national networks or 'focal points' within each country or resource organization. For example, it has been suggested that workshop announcements should be sent only to one person in the national network who would then be responsible for national dissemination and communications.

However, practical experience has shown that restricting information flows in this way may not always be reliable. Key individuals and institutions may at one time be facilitators and at other times (unintentionally) communications bottlenecks. There have been examples of national networks or focal points forgetting to pass on announcements, letters or publications. Some people have been too embarrassed to mention they have had no money for local postage.

Furthermore, network members can, with little or no warning, be promoted to a different post, sent on study leave or incapacitated by illness or accident. Within national and international institutions, managements can change or shift priorities, work loads can suddenly increase, key staff leave and budgets be cut. In such circumstances, network correspondence can be neglected. This may not be too critical if just one individual or organization is involved, but if other network members rely on that focal point to disseminate information, they could be deprived.

Where communications are rapid and feedback is expected, networkers can often work out from lack of response that there has been an information blockage. In other circumstances, it may take months to know that information is not being disseminated and people may lose the chance to participate in an important event.

Thus, a 'belt and braces' approach to information exchange appears most effective. Focal points may be useful, but they should not be used exclusively for important information dissemination unless there is a system of rapid feedback.

Seeing the benefits

While all those associated with the networks can point to the advantages of improved knowledge and understanding to individuals and programmes, it is extremely difficult to measure the benefits.

If one looks back to the years of work wasted in the past on unsuitable technologies in Africa (such as wheeled toolcarriers which were 'perfected yet rejected'), one can see the great potential for savings through networking. This does not just apply to hardware. For example, one project in West Africa spent two million dollars attempting to introduce Asian water buffaloes for rice cultivation in northern Senegal. The project did not interact with colleagues familiar with other attempts to introduce exotic work animals into sub-Saharan Africa. The money would have been better utilized had those responsible for planning and implementation been exposed to the experiences and perspectives of network members.

Other comparable recent project initiatives may well have already been made more relevant and productive because people have been able to learn from the animal traction networks. It is impossible to know how many programmes and projects have benefited, but some clear examples of network influence can be documented.

A clear example of benefits

To illustrate the genuine yet elusive nature of the benefits, one can take the example of an animal traction project in Guinea.

The leaders of this project made use of some publications of the West Africa network to learn of and then to contact colleagues working in Mali, Senegal and Sierra Leone. This led to one three-week training visit to Mali and the testing of Senegalese and Sierra Leonean implements in Guinea. It also resulted in detailed discussions on technical, economic and organizational issues and to the project obtaining

networking for
development

75

documents on a wide variety of topics. Moreover, each contact led to others: for example, the people in Mali were able to discuss the experiences of their colleagues in Togo, whom they had met at a workshop.

Such information exchange would have been almost impossible a mere five years before, simply because people in one country were almost completely unaware of each other's activities. As a result of its networking and dynamism, the project implemented some well-proven strategies, and so achieved in two years an output that, in more 'normal' circumstances, might well have taken three to four years. It is arguable that in this one case, at least one year of project time (a quantifiable figure) was saved through networking. There must be numerous other comparable cases, with total potential savings of millions of dollars.

In practice, it is always difficult to prove specific financial savings have come from networking alone. While all involved in the Guinea project believed they saved time and money, it would be difficult to objectively prove a cause and effect relationship. Many other factors were also involved.

It is difficult to measure the specific economic benefits. The 'time saved' cannot be reliably quantified without a 'control' for comparison (which is impossible). Similarly, while the genuine value of networking in the region can be seen in the improvements in knowledge, understanding and programme implementation, it will remain difficult to estimate the total benefits.

Resources

The animal traction networks do not require huge budgets or luxurious facilities, but they do need resources to operate efficiently. For most of their existence, the international networks have had no financial resources of their own, and no central budget or account. All the day-to-day costs of networking have been met by individuals or their parent institutions. The introduction of workshop fees has provided networks with a small amount of money to allow them to cover operational costs between workshops.

Sufficient funds can generally be obtained for specific activities such as workshops and study tours. When these are arranged, network members (organizers and participants)

have generally been able to claim relevant expenditure from the workshop account or one of the sponsoring organizations.

Nonetheless, most activities have been organized in faith, with expenditure coming long before a refund. This has placed considerable financial strain on some individuals and organizations trying to facilitate the activities.

Fickle resource organizations

Certain resource organizations have tended to be fickle: sometimes supporting the networks strongly, sometimes appearing rather cool. Such inconsistencies may have been due to alterations in institutional policy, to deteriorating budgetary situations within the organizations, or to the changing whims of particular individuals.

Whatever the stated position of a resource organization, practical support for the networks has depended largely on the enthusiasm of one, or more, key individuals. Whether an activity is supported or not depends to a large extent on the prevailing work load, mood or self-interest of the contact individual. While formal applications are always necessary, the real decision whether or not to fund an activity may be taken during an initial telephone call or personal visit. Much depends on the perceived track record of the network, and the individuals involved.

User support

At all the international workshops held so far, the majority of participants have been funded from sources within their own countries. In practice, such support has come mainly from local donor-assisted projects. This has made workshop organization easier and cheaper. It has also emphasized the user-supported nature of the networks and demonstrated the potential sustainability of network activities. When applications for sponsorship have been received by the committee organizing a workshop, people have been actively encouraged to obtain local sponsorship. It has often been possible to put that applicant in touch with a sponsoring agency within his or her country, so initiating useful and beneficial contacts.

The national and international networks have been run on a voluntary basis. When activities, such as workshops, have been organized, or papers written and edited, the host institutions have given permission for their staff to spend time on these jobs. However, they have not reduced their other work loads, and individuals have often been quite stressed.

The work of the networks' technical adviser (the author of this book) has also been largely on a voluntary basis, with no budget for the time and communication costs involved in network activities. For some major organizational or editorial tasks, sponsoring agencies have provided short-term consultancy assignments.

Limits to user support

While it has been shown that network members and their organizations are generally willing and able to provide their own time to plan and implement activities, there are limits to this. If very high demands are made (for example, organizing a large workshop or preparing a publication) it may be necessary for a person to take leave and receive some salary compensation for the assignment.

International networking costs, including telecommunications, airmail postage of documents and air travel rapidly mount up. Only resource-rich organizations can afford such expenses. If foreign exchange is required, even fewer organizations can participate easily.

For active, long-distance international networking, access to resources is needed, whether from a local organization or from a workshop budget. However, even if such resources are difficult to obtain, scope may exist for cheaper land-based networking with neighbouring countries, at costs comparable to those of national networking.

Resources for national-level networking

National-level networking activities can generally be funded locally. Members working with donor-assisted programmes often find national networking straightforward. They can obtain funds for local travel and subsistence and so can readily attend meetings and workshops.

Unfortunately many Africa-based organizations concerned with animal traction (including some universities and ministry departments) have very limited facilities. Their budgets tend to be so dominated by personnel costs that little remains for operational expenditure. In such cases network members find local transport, document reproduction and communications costs hard to obtain. They also find it difficult to travel to meetings and workshops unless some other agency is willing to sponsor them.

Thus, even at the national level, there is a large disparity in people's financial ability to network effectively. The national animal traction networks have generally depended on their association with local resource-rich programmes or donor agencies in order to hold meetings and workshops and to publish newsletters and proceedings. Without such assistance they would either fail to operate or would become merely élite associations.

Resources for major workshops and publications

It has proved relatively easy to attract donor funds for major international workshops (although each activity has required considerable volunteered time and communications costs to solicit the support). Similarly, donor assistance has been offered for publications and for particular work assignments (such as preparation of proceedings). The good 'track record' of international network publications has been important in securing the continued support of donor agencies.

All the national networks have secured funds for at least one local workshop. Donor agencies have tended to be reluctant to support follow-up activities unless there have been demonstrable outputs and benefits from the initial workshop(s).

Funding network planning and coordination

It has not proved easy to attract funds for general network planning and coordination. The networks have often had to rely on the (volunteered) services of steering committee representatives and the network technical adviser to undertake planning and liaison duties between events.

networking for
development

79

Meetings of the steering committees have had to be organized on an *ad hoc* basis, when funds or opportunities have been available. It has not helped committee morale, commitment and professionalism to end meetings without knowing if, and when, they would be able to meet again.

In 1992, a proposal to a donor agency to fund an ATNESA steering committee planning meeting was declined by an official who indicated that his ministry did not wish to support 'jet setting'. At that time the network had not achieved sufficient respect and legitimacy within his organization. In practice, the value and effectiveness of professional travel depends entirely on the particular organizations and individuals concerned (the implied accusation of that donor agency representative seems to have been based on an irregular verb: I undertake essential work travel; you combine business and pleasure; they are jet setting ...!).

The probable benefits of any planned travel can only be judged by reference to the people involved and past experience. The actual benefits can only be seen in the light of the meetings' outputs and subsequent achievements. As the network's outputs become clearer, it should be easier to convince donors that the steering committee members are responsible and serious and that their meetings warrant support.

To coordinate, develop and participate in a democratic international network requires communications, planning meetings and international travel. While electronic communications can improve international liaison, some joint planning meetings are essential. If external or core funding is not available, only people from resource-rich organizations can participate in meetings and activities. Members working in less affluent organizations effectively become ineligible for network participation and membership of a steering committee.

Networks should therefore attempt to obtain modest core funding for the essential steering committee activities of network planning, coordination and delegation. Such provision should supplement voluntary work, user support and specific activity funding.

Banking and institutional association

Both international networks experienced problems in establishing central bank accounts. Firstly, neither network was a legally established entity. Secondly, it was difficult to find a bank that would allow low-cost international money transfers within the region. In several countries, foreign exchange restrictions and high rates of inflation made it difficult and undesirable to deposit donor-supplied funds into local bank accounts. Other international networks, professional associations and regional NGOs have experienced similar problems, although the recent trend in Africa towards the liberalization of foreign exchange regulations should improve the situation in future. To date, donor funds received for the activities of the international networks have been administered through supporting resource organizations, national host institutions or individuals contracted to the relevant donors.

One option available to international networks is to establish accounts in association with a sympathetic international institution, donor agency or NGO. However, the accountants of such organizations tend to be reluctant to handle third-party funds. Legally established national networks do not face the same problem. Informal networks have generally benefited from association with one of their supporting organizations.

Legitimacy and public awareness

The international animal traction networks have gained regional and international recognition and legitimacy through their activities, publicity and publications. As legitimacy increases, the international networks will have more influence on the policies of national governments, regional groupings and donor agencies. Already there is evidence that some actions and policies of local organizations, national institutions or international agencies have been modified by citing the concerns of the international networks or referring to their publications and policies.

National networks are often in a good position to influence policies, particularly if national institutions identify themselves with the networks. National networks with clear identity, activities and outputs are most likely to achieve influence and legitimacy.

networking for development

Network logos and names

Logos have been extremely useful in creating awareness and recognition. The international network logos have combined regional map outlines with illustrations of the animal traction technologies (see pages 51 and 56). Although the logos are relatively complicated they clearly illustrate the diversity of animal traction (involving oxen and donkeys, men and women, tillage and transport). Most national network logos have similarly combined national map outlines with examples of animal traction.

There has been some debate as to whether the networks should refer to 'animal traction', 'animal draft/draught' or 'animal power'. Unfortunately the term 'animal traction' is not always immediately understood by people outside agricultural development circles. Also, some people think that the term traction (associated with pulling) neglects the importance of animals for carrying. But no alternative is entirely satisfactory. The words for 'animal traction' are very similar in French, English, Spanish and Portuguese and all international networks use 'animal traction'. In the circumstances, it seems sensible for the networks to retain their names and use effective publicity (and logos) to make sure people clearly understand what the term means.

While network acronyms can be promoted as useful names (e.g. ATNESA, KENDAT, SANAT), it is less advisable to use unfamiliar acronyms in network publicity documents. Acronyms such as AT, DAT, DAP (animal traction, draft animal technology, draft animal power) are not well-known, and tend to give new readers the impression of jargon and exclusivity.

Having achieved useful international recognition, it would be most unfortunate for the networks to lose their names and identities as a result of formal association with other organizations. As long as there are clear requirements for multidisciplinary, multifunctional animal traction networks, these should exist and be clearly recognizable.

Influence on policies

networking for
development

82

To date, the international networks have concentrated on information exchange. It has been up to individual members and the national networks to influence policies within their own countries.

While the overall policy environment relating to animal traction is much more favourable than it was in the 1960s, 70s and 80s, many problems remain. For example, governments and donor agencies still tend to give undue emphasis and resources to schemes to promote tractorization (rather than animal traction), meat production from cattle (rather than multipurpose and animal power functions), oxen (rather than cows or donkeys), imported or centrally-produced implements (rather than decentralized, local production) and male-dominated animal traction systems (rather than animal traction for women).

The international steering committees and network working groups might now consider whether, and how, the networks could start to have more influence on policy. This could become a sensitive issue, because if the networks were to become more active as pressure groups, they might appear to challenge some of the preconceptions of national policy makers and donor agencies. A subtle approach is therefore likely to be appropriate, with the international networks assisting their members to achieve agreed policy objectives through circulation of network policy papers, targeted publicity and strategic workshops.

Raising professional standards

One role of the networks is to enhance the skills and raise the professional standards of their members. For the multidisciplinary, multifunctional animal traction networks, the relevant professional knowledge, skills and training cover a very wide range: for example, from improving experimental research techniques to understanding the gender biases implicit in certain farming systems.

Network leadership in improving communication skills seems particularly appropriate, as most members, whether researchers, extension agents or leaders of farmers' groups, need to express themselves well at meetings and in papers, reports and proposals.

The networks have already made efforts in this area, and there is some evidence that standards are rising although, as with all improvements over time, it is difficult to ascribe precise cause and effect relationships. Detailed guidelines on paper preparation and presentation have been circulated before all workshops, and many members have made an

networking for
development

83

effort to conform to the requested standards. The proportion of papers submitted to workshops that include abstracts and full details of references cited has increased. The use of visual aids (slides and overhead sheets) has also improved, and more workshop participants come with clear poster displays.

The standards set by the published network proceedings, the participatory methodology of workshops and the professional discipline of formal workshop presentations appear also to have influenced the quality of national publications and local workshops.

Training needs

Despite rising standards, there is still a clear need for further assistance to help members improve their skills in writing, presentations and proposal formulation. There is a marked disparity between 'international' network members (who have often studied abroad and/or participated in other international events) and those whose experiences have been largely based in the rural areas of their home countries.

Although the work of most network members concerns farmers, few people have received training in open-ended farmer interviews or rapid rural appraisal techniques. As a result, some network researchers still try to obtain information entirely through fixed response surveys implemented by enumerators.

The network steering committees (national and international) might consider ways in which their members could be assisted further. For example, guidelines could be prepared relating to workshop presentations, project proposals, research protocols and rapid rural appraisal surveys. Specific training workshops could be held (ILCA once arranged a workshop on animal traction research protocols for West African members). Relevant resource persons could be brought in to assist members during network events and special training sessions could be held during, or immediately before, workshops. Professional editors have attended several ATNESA workshops to assist people with their papers, and this service has been very favourably received according to workshop evaluations.

Many of the communication skills referred to here are not specific to animal traction. Other networks are also concerned with raising professional standards, and so there is much scope for exchanges of experience and cooperation with other networks and resource organizations in relation to training and publication of guidelines.

Newsletters and information sources

The international and national networks would all like to have regular newsletters. Newsletters have undoubted value, but they require considerable resources: not only the costs of printing and distribution, but also editorial time. Editors have to write articles themselves based on information received and also to solicit contributions from members. Many networks and organizations know how difficult it is to sustain newsletters after the first few exciting new issues, or after the initial donor-supplied funds have been spent.

The Centre for Tropical Veterinary Medicine of the University of Edinburgh has been publishing the newsletter *Draught Animal News* since 1983. This has regularly contained contributions from the networks' members and information about network events. Many other newsletters and information sources on tropical agriculture, appropriate technology and related subjects sometimes include information relating to animal traction and the networks. These newsletters, combined with the networks' formal publications, already provide an important information base.

This does not imply that further network newsletters would not be desirable. The interest generated by the national animal traction newsletters of Togo, Zambia and South Africa shows what an impact newsletters can have. However, additional newsletter production should not be an urgent priority.

In the short term, steering committees would do well to encourage their members to receive and contribute to other relevant newsletters. They might also consider more formal arrangements with sympathetic newsletters for regular columns or pages relating to their networks.

networking for
development

Linkages with other networks

The national and international networks have made considerable efforts to work closely with other relevant networks of national, regional and international scope. All the main workshops arranged by national networks have been attended by invited participants from neighbouring countries and/or the international networks.

The international networks have circulated their announcements and publications to a large number of networks and organizations in Africa, the Americas, Asia, Australia and Europe.

There has been close cooperation between WAATN and ATNESA. The formation of ATNESA was stimulated by the activities of WAATN. Subsequently, committee members of the West Africa network have attended ATNESA workshops (both large and thematic).

The networks have also invited representatives of other networks and organizations to their events. There have been close links with regional farming systems networks, the Network for Agricultural Mechanization in Africa (NAMA) and the International Forum for Rural Transport and Development (IFRTD). ATNESA members have collaborated with other agencies in holding small animal traction workshops on themes of particular interest to those organizations.

Although there are several partner networks with overlapping interests (notably the farming systems, mechanization, cattle and rural transport networks) none is in direct competition and there have been no signs of intolerance. In general, inter-network linkages appear to be very good and should be maintained through mailing lists, exchange of publications and invitations to workshops and planning meetings.

Network linkages could be further strengthened through joint activities such as thematic workshops or professional training courses on topics of mutual interest.

Farmer involvement

International networking

Both international animal traction networks claim to have farming systems perspectives and aim to be farmer-orientated. Although farmers and farmers' groups are eligible to be members, both networks have been dominated by public sector employees working for organizations concerned with research, development, extension, education, training, infrastructural support and the management of aid programmes.

This is not unexpected, for the target group for membership is those working to assist the farmers, rather than farmers themselves. The farmers are the intended long-term beneficiaries, but in the short term the networks expect to improve national and local programmes.

The network steering committees have discussed the issue of farmer involvement, and have concluded that members operating at national and local levels should be encouraged to involve smallholder farmers in their activities but that active farmer participation in the international networks would be highly problematic.

The international networks have included small-group, village-based discussions with farmers as central elements of their workshops. These have influenced subsequent debate, and participants sounding too theoretical have been reminded by colleagues about the real problems experienced by farmers using animal traction.

National networking

Many national network members work very closely with farmers (although there are some with little direct contact). Several members commonly arrange or facilitate local or provincial meetings to allow farmers to discuss aspects of animal traction technology. The results and implications of such farmer contact should be communicated to the national and international networks through workshop participation and report circulation by the agriculturalists involved.

Some national networks including those in Kenya, Tanzania, South Africa and Zambia have obtained more direct feedback by inviting farmers to local workshops. This

networking for development

has often resulted in some highly educational and productive discussions.

Although farmer participation can have great value, it can also cause organizational problems at formal workshops. Many 'typical' farmers are unrelaxed in a workshop environment dominated by civil servants. Their vernacular may require translation; they may prefer to talk at length on general issues rather than synthesize their animal traction problems. Farmers who are relaxed and able to express themselves in a focused way are likely to be atypical, and may be more involved in commerce or local politics than farming. Their problems may not be the same as their neighbouring small farmers, whether men or women, and yet their cases may dominate workshop discussions. In general, farmers contribute best, and participants learn most, if the farmers (and their entire farming households) are in their own environments during discussions.

Farmer workshops on animal traction

One way of avoiding the problem of traditional farmers appearing 'out of place' in a professional workshop environment is to arrange workshops that are dominated by farmers rather than researchers or extensionists.

The Guinean animal traction network (Réseau Guinéen sur la Traction Animale) has held national workshops for farmers from different provinces and ethnic groups to discuss their problems, successes and needs. The emphasis has been on farmer-to-farmer discussions in small groups, wherever possible in the local vernaculars. Such workshops have involved considerable organization in terms of transport arrangements, food, lodging and participant synchronization. They have also required skill and sensitivity in orientating discussions and facilitating timely reporting. However, they have proved extremely valuable in problem identification, farmer-to-farmer suggestions and technology transfer. Similar workshops for blacksmiths have also been held.

Other networks might well consider the Guinean methodology and experiences. Similar events involving farmers from more than one country might also be facilitated.

Farmer-to-farmer transfer of technology

Many research and development workers have tended to think in terms of transfer of technology through formal extension programmes. However, there is evidence that many animal traction technologies have been transferred from farmer to farmer, or blacksmith to blacksmith. Transfer between countries also occurs through farmer-to-farmer contacts. There have also been examples of project-arranged exchanges of farmers and blacksmiths leading to the transfer of animal traction technologies.

The national and international network steering committees might therefore consider whether other farmer-to-farmer visits between countries would be useful and cost-effective, and how they might be arranged.

Women farmers

The importance of women farmers is being increasingly recognized. Nevertheless most development organizations, including the national and international animal traction networks, tend to be male-dominated. It would be helpful if the steering committees considered how to increase the involvement of women farmers and network members in future network activities.

Monitoring and evaluation

None of the animal traction networks has developed any formal or informal means for monitoring and evaluating overall progress. This is not surprising as few networks anywhere in the world have given much attention to this.

A network is not a goal, but a means of achieving a goal. The effectiveness of a steering committee (or secretariat) has to be judged not by narrowly-defined immediate targets (meetings, workshops, publications) but by the achievements of others.

The very consideration of possible means of monitoring and evaluation is likely to prove a valuable planning exercise to the network core groups. All animal traction network steering committees (or national coordinating bodies) should take time to discuss the relevance and practicalities of monitoring and evaluating their networks.

networking for development

Donor agencies might well favourably consider funding one or more specific studies in this area. One study might concern the impact of networking on animal traction in Africa. Another might relate to the potential value of goal-orientated planning for the animal traction networks.

The results of studies such as these (whether or not the overall conclusions are positive or negative) should prove very valuable for future network planning and the submission of funding proposals. As the discussions and studies are likely to be of great interest to other, similar networks, there may well be potential for inter-network cooperation and linkages in these areas.

Other practical problems

Languages

The main official, international languages in sub-Saharan Africa are English, French and Portuguese. Since Portuguese is only spoken in a few countries, internationally-oriented people in Portuguese-speaking countries generally make an effort to learn English or French. This is much less true in anglophone and francophone Africa, where it is still quite rare to find people fluent in both languages. Such language barriers raise problems for networking.

Many anglophone and francophone people can read documents in the other language. This makes individual networking by mail feasible, if people write in their own language, and expect a reply in another. However, people of both language groups expect official network documents to be available in their own language, as a question of principle. This increases the effort and cost of network communications.

Face to face meetings can be problematic, particularly if detailed discussions are required. Simultaneous translation is very expensive (it can double the cost of organizing a workshop). Single language meetings and workshops are exclusive, and restrict international exchanges. ATNESA operates in a mainly anglophone region, and has been able to justify English-only workshops. In West Africa, the situation is more difficult and sensitive. Some of the problems of the West Africa network have been exacerbated by the lack of bilingualism among steering committee members and partner organizations.

Post and telecommunications

Postal services and telecommunications between African countries can be very slow, difficult and unreliable. Indeed because intra-Africa communications can be difficult compared to Europe-Africa links, it has sometimes proved more practical to communicate via Europe. Although this was not planned, the fact that the network technical adviser has an office in Europe has frequently proved invaluable in facilitating network liaison and information dissemination.

E-mail

The increasing use of e-mail in Africa is beginning to help the networks. Communication between committee members has been greatly improved. Some workshop announcements are sent by e-mail and some registrations and papers are now submitted by e-mail. Papers and planning documents can be rapidly worked on by teams of people in different countries, and finalized in less time than it would have taken to post out the first draft.

However, only a small minority of members have access to e-mail. It is generally those from resource-rich, urban-based organizations who can contact each other by e-mail rapidly and cheaply. These people are therefore the first to receive information and the first to react. Informal 'inner committees' have developed within steering committees, with those on e-mail communicating regularly leaving the others unintentionally excluded and marginalized. Members working with farmers in remote rural areas still often have to wait weeks for normal mail. Thus e-mail is emphasizing the increasing disparity in communication facilities.

Despite the many problems of e-mail, this technology has huge potential to assist networks. All networks operating in countries where e-mail is available and affordable should seriously consider how they could benefit from electronic communications. For example, collaborating groups (network boards, workshop organizing committees, publication editors) might well make efforts to ensure all members have e-mail addresses, so allowing easy, rapid communications.

networking for development

91

Air schedules and meetings

Air schedules and connections within Africa are such that committee members or workshop participants can seldom all arrive and depart on the same day. Two or even three days may be needed for air travel between some countries. Thus attendance at a three-day meeting may require people to sacrifice a week from their work. Difficult air schedules can significantly increase meeting costs, as provision has to be made for additional *per diem* payments.

It has proved very difficult to bring together all members of the steering committees at the same time. In 1990-91 there were three separate meetings of the WAATN steering committee, but at none of these did the committee members feel that enough members were present to make binding decisions about the future organization of the network. At each meeting, one or more of the individuals crucial to the topic under discussion were unavoidably absent due to conflicting activities, communication difficulties, travel problems, illness, political upheavals or other unforeseen circumstances.

Technology already exists to make to make e-mail discussions and virtual committee meetings possible. It may be that international networks will have to make use of such communications systems, to obtain consensus. However, such systems will never surpass the advantages of informal, face-to-face discussions during farm visits.

Work pressures, conflicts

During workshops and meetings, network members can devote themselves fully to network activities. In the enthusiasm of a workshop, participants find it easy to offer to take on responsibilities. However, well-meant intentions to assist network activities tend to be relegated to the background when members return to their families, and to their own demanding jobs. Furthermore, not all members who participate in international events involve themselves in national networking activities.

Publication delays

The rapid publication of workshop proceedings has been an aim of both the regional and the national networks. In practice this has proved difficult. Most major edited proceedings have taken at least two years to produce, and sometimes three or more years. National proceedings with fewer papers and less rigorous standards have generally taken from eight to 18 months. The delegation of responsibilities to different organizations and editors has confirmed that the problem is not limited to any one organization or individual. However, publication delays have been frustrating to the workshop participants, network members and funding organizations.

Network inbreeding

One danger with any network is the tendency for it to become 'inbred'. The animal traction field is quite small, both nationally and internationally. When colleagues meet each other frequently, familiarity tends to diminish the intensity of technical communication. One way of avoiding this pitfall has been to attract many new people to each workshop by arranging large, open workshops. However, large events are not always appropriate, and networks may have to encourage individual core members not to participate in every network event. Workshops could become stale if they did so.

Conclusions

There has been a huge change in information exchange relating to animal traction in Africa in recent years, much of which is directly, or indirectly, attributable to the activities of the animal traction networks. There is also increasing collaboration between programmes, notably in the areas of research, training and implement testing. The international and national animal traction networks have achieved a great deal through their workshops, publications, professional support and the raising of awareness. The value and cost effectiveness of networking has been clearly demonstrated, whether it be international or national, and whether formal or informal.

Whatever the structure and organization of a network, the main thing is that active networking takes place. Animal traction networks need to encourage broad participation and decentralized initiatives. Network core groups need to evolve and develop processes to stimulate active networking between other network members. An enthusiastic and facilitating approach to network coordination involving both delegation and rigorous monitoring is likely to be

networking for development

most effective. Although secretariats and newsletters may be highly desirable they are expensive and difficult to sustain. Networks can be very effective on low overheads, building on member interest, voluntary work and delegated responsibilities. However they do need adequate resources to ensure interaction.

Concrete activities are required to maintain network interest. These should relate to the areas of high priority of network members and the users of animal traction. Network events that combine participatory processes, farmer-orientated activities and clear outputs will continue to be important. While the large general workshops will remain popular, particularly for those for whom they are a completely new experience, it is probable that the international networks will put increasing efforts into more focused events for special interest groups. For example, intensive seminars may be held for researchers working on similar topics (e.g. the use of draft cows) or for development projects involved in similar work (e.g. the use of animal traction for rice production) or for the people working with artisanal manufacturers or small-scale transporters. Such activities can continue to be hosted and organized by national networks and associated organizations, perhaps in collaboration with other networks.

It is likely that the combination of member enthusiasm, open membership, flexible communication channels and multi-donor support will ensure the continuing effectiveness of the African animal traction networks. With appropriate support, present and future animal traction networks will be able to work at national, regional and international levels to assist and promote the development of animal traction in sustainable agricultural and transport systems in Africa into the next century.

networking for development

APPENDIX 1: FURTHER READING

General networking and network examples

Alders C, Haverkort B and van Veldhuizen L (eds), 1993. *Linking with farmers: networking for low-external-input and sustainable agriculture.* Intermediate Technology Publications, London, UK. 298pp. ISBN 1-85339-210-3

GATE, 1992. Networking: lessons and hopes. *GATE questions, answers, information* 4/92. German Appropriate Technology Exchange (GATE), Eschborn, Germany. 56pp. ISSN 0723-2225

ILEIA, 1992. Let's work together. *ILEIA Newsletter* 2/92. Information Centre for Low External Input and Sustainable Agriculture (ILEIA), Leusden, The Netherlands. 48pp. ISSN 0920-8771

Moelinono I and Fisher L, 1992. Networking for development: some experiences and observations. pp. 217-223 in: *Networking for LEISA.* Background reader prepared for workshop held 9-15 March 1992, Silang, Philippines. Information Centre for Low External Input and Sustainable Agriculture (ILEIA), Leusden, The Netherlands.

Nelson J and Farrington J, 1994. *Information exchange networks for agricultural development: a review of concepts and practices.* Technical Centre for Agriculture and Rural Cooperation (CTA), Ede-Wageningen, The Netherlands. 86pp. ISBN 92-9081-1137

Starkey P, 1996. *Networking for sustainable agriculture: lessons from animal traction development.* Gatekeeper Series 58, International Institute for Environment and Development (IIED), London, UK. 18pp. ISSN: 1357-9258

Animal traction networking

Bwalya M and de Graaf J, 1992. *Animal traction in agricultural development.* Proceedings of a workshop held 27-29 May 1992, Lusaka, Zambia. Palabana Animal Draft Power Development Programme, Lusaka, Zambia. 45pp.

networking for development

95

Dennis R A (ed), 1996. *Guidelines for design, production and testing of animal-drawn carts.* Published for Animal Traction Network for Eastern and Southern Africa (ATNESA) by IT Publications, London, UK. 187pp. ISBN 1 85339 338 X.

FAO, 1984. *Animal energy in agriculture in Africa and Asia.* Animal Production and Health Paper No. 42, Food and Agriculture Organization (FAO), Rome, Italy. 143pp.

Imboden R, Starkey P H and Goe M R, 1983. *Report of the preparatory consultation mission for the establishment of a TCDC network for research, training and development of draught animal power in Africa.* AGA Consultancy Report, Food and Agriculture Organization (FAO), Rome, Italy. 115pp.

Kalisky J (ed), 1990. *Proceedings of a regional course on planning an integrated animal draught programme,* held Harare, Zimbabwe from 5-13 November 1990. Bulletin No. 2. Agricultural Operations Technology for Smallholders in East and Southern Africa (AGROTEC), Harare, Zimbabwe. 235pp.

Kanali C L, Okello P O, Wasike B S and Klapwijk M, 1993. *Improving draught animal technology.* Proceedings of the first conference of the Kenya Network for Draught Animal Technology (KENDAT) held 3-6 November 1992, Nairobi, Kenya. KENDAT, University of Nairobi, Kenya. 124pp.

Kaumbutho P G *et al* (eds), 1996. *Meeting the challenges of draught animal technologies in Kenya.* Proceedings of the second KENDAT national workshop held 27-31 March 1995, Karen, Kenya. Kenya Network for Draught Animal Technology (KENDAT), University of Nairobi, Kenya. 61pp.

Lawrence P R, Lawrence K, Dijkman J T and Starkey P H (eds), 1993. *Research for development of animal traction in West Africa.* Proceedings of the fourth workshop of the West Africa Animal Traction Network held 9-13 July 1990, Kano, Nigeria. International Livestock Centre for Africa (ILCA), Addis Ababa, Ethiopia. 322pp. ISBN 92-9053-276-9

Mejía Gómez J and Granda Jimbo D (eds) 1996. *La tracción animal y desarrollo sostenible*. Memorias de Primer Encuento Centroamericano de Tracción Animal, Managua, November 1995. FOMENTA, Managua, Nicaragua. 150pp.

MoA, 1994. *Proceedings of the first national workshop on animal traction technology in Ethiopia (27-28 January 1994)*. Land Use Study and Rural Technology Promotion Department, Ministry of Agriculture (MoA), Addis Ababa, Ethiopia. 64pp.

Namponya C R (ed), 1988. *Animal traction and agricultural mechanization research in SADCC member countries*. Proceedings of workshop held August 1987, Maputo, Mozambique. SACCAR Workshop Series 7, Southern African Centre for Cooperation in Agricultural Research (SACCAR), Gaborone, Botswana. 87pp.

Shetto R M, Kwiligwa E M and Simalenga T E (eds), 1994. *Proceedings of a regional workshop on implements for field crop production and transportation systems on smallholders farms,* held Dar es Salaam, Tanzania from 15-19 November 1993. Agricultural Operations Technology for Smallholders in East and Southern Africa (AGROTEC), Harare, Zimbabwe. 94pp.

Simalenga T E and Hatibu N (eds), 1991. *Proceedings of an animal traction workshop held 8-10 April 1991, Morogoro, Tanzania*. Mbeya Oxenization Project, Mbeya, Tanzania. 57pp.

Simalenga T E and Joubert A B D (eds), 1997. *Animal traction in South Africa: today and tomorrow*. Proceedings of the SANAT workshop held 26-28 March 1996. South Africa Network for Animal Traction (SANAT), University of Fort Hare, Alice, South Africa. 82pp.

Simalenga T and Kalisky J (eds), 1993. Proceedings of a regional workshop on design, manufacture, testing and standardization of animal-drawn implements, held Harare, Zimbabwe from 7-11 December 1992. *Bulletin No. 8*. Agricultural Operations Technology for Smallholders in East and Southern Africa (AGROTEC), Harare, Zimbabwe. 108pp.

networking for development

Starkey P, 1988. *Perfected yet rejected: animal-drawn wheeled toolcarriers.* Vieweg for German Appropriate Technology Exchange, GTZ, Eschborn, Germany. 161pp. ISBN 3-528-02053-9

Starkey P, 1991. *The revival of animal traction in Kindia Region of Guinea Conakry* (Relance de la traction bovine dans la région de Kindia, Guinée Conakry). Report of evaluation of project ONG/78/89/B Guinea Conakry. Commission of the European Communities, Brussels, Belgium. 43pp.

Starkey P, 1992. *Networking for animal traction.* Network Discussion Paper 1/92. Animal Traction Network for Eastern and Southern Africa (ATNESA) and West Africa Animal Traction Network (WAATN). GTZ, Eschborn, Germany. 45pp.

Starkey P, 1995 (ed). *Animal power in South Africa: empowering rural communities.* Development Bank of Southern Africa, Gauteng, South Africa. 160pp. ISBN 1-874878-67-6

Starkey P and Faye A (eds), 1990. *Animal traction for agricultural development.* Proceedings of the Third Regional Workshop of the West Africa Animal Traction Network, held 7-12 July 1988, Saly, Senegal. Technical Centre for Agricultural and Rural Cooperation (CTA), Ede-Wageningen, Netherlands. 475pp. ISBN 92-9081-046-7

Starkey P and Goe M R, 1984 and 1995. *Report of an FAO/ILCA mission to prepare for the establishment of a TCDC network for research, training and development of draught animal power in Africa.* AGA Consultancy Report, Food and Agriculture Organization (FAO), Rome, Italy. 82pp./85pp.

Starkey P and Ndiamé F (eds), 1988. *Animal power in farming systems.* Proceedings of workshop held 17-26 September 1986, Freetown, Sierra Leone. Vieweg for German Appropriate Technology Exchange, GTZ, Eschborn, Germany. 363pp. ISBN 3-528-02047-4

Starkey P, Mwenya E and Stares J (eds), 1994. *Improving animal traction technology.* Proceedings of Animal Traction Network for Eastern and Southern Africa (ATNESA) workshop held 18-23 January 1992, Lusaka, Zambia. Technical Centre for Agricultural and Rural Cooperation (CTA), Ede-Wageningen, The Netherlands. 496pp. ISBN: 92-9081-127-7

Starkey P, Simalenga T and Miller F, 1997. *Animal power for weed control. Proceedings of a workshop held 1-5 November 1993, Tanga, Tanzania.* Animal Traction Network for Eastern and Southern Africa (ATNESA) and Technical Centre for Agricultural and Rural Cooperation (CTA), Ede-Wageningen, The Netherlands. 256pp. ISBN 92-9081-136-6 (in press).

Starkey P *et al* (eds), 1996. *Meeting the challenges of animal traction.* Report of the workshop of the Animal Traction Network for Eastern and Southern Africa (ATNESA) held 4-8 December 1995, Karen, Kenya. Animal Traction Development, Reading, UK. 56pp.

Sylwander L and Mpande R (eds), 1995. *Gender issues in animal traction.* Guidelines for programmes from a workshop held 1-5 June 1992, Mbeya, Tanzania. Animal Traction Network for Eastern and Southern Africa (ATNESA), Harare, Zimbabwe. 60pp.

networking for
development

APPENDIX 2: NETWORK CONTACTS

Animal traction networks

ATNESA Secretariat and Animal Power Network for Zimbabwe (APNEZ) (Attn Ms Bertha MUDAMBURI)
Agritex Institute of Agricultural Engineering
Box BW 330, Borrowdale, Harare, ZIMBABWE
Tel: + 263-4-860019
Fax:+ 263-4-860136
E-mail: atnesa@interzim.icon.co.zw

ATNESA Chair (Dr T E SIMALENGA)
University of Fort Hare, Faculty of Agriculture
Private Bag X1314, Alice 5700, SOUTH AFRICA
Tel: + 27-4060-22232
Fax: + 27-4065-31730
E-mail: TIM.S@ufhcc.ufh.ac.za

ATNESA Technical Adviser (Professor Paul STARKEY)
Animal Traction Development
Oxgate, 64 Northcourt Ave, Reading RG2 7HQ, UK
Tel: + 44-118-9872152
Fax: + 44-118-9314525
E-mail: P.H.Starkey@reading.ac.uk

Ethiopian Network of Animal Traction (ENAT)
(Attn Dr ALEMU Gebre Wold and Ato FRIEW Kelemu)
Institute of Agricultural Research (IAR)
PO Box 2003, Addis Ababa. ETHIOPIA
Tel: + 251-1-511802   Fax: + 251-1-611222
E-mail: IAR@telecom.net.et

Kenya Network for Draught Animal Technology (KENDAT)
(Attn Dr Pascal KAUMBUTHO)
Department of Agricultural Engineering
University of Nairobi, Box 30197, Nairobi, KENYA
Tel/Fax: + 254-2-593465
E-mail: Kendat@ken.healthnet.org

networking for development

100

Projet pour la Promotion de la Traction Animale (PROPTA)
(Attn Dr Kossivi APETOFIA)
BP 37, Atakpamé, TOGO
Tel: + 228-400204   Fax: + 228-400411, 400033

Red Latinoamericana de Tracción Animal (RELATA)
FOMENTA
Apdo 95 Telcor Douglas Mejía, Managua,
NICARAGUA
Tel: + 505-266-4084   Fax: + 505-266-8617
E-mail: relata@ibw.com.ni

Réseau Guinéen sur la Traction Animale (RGTA)
(Attn Dr Almamy Sény SOUMAH)
BP 148, Kindia, GUINEA CONAKRY
Tel: + 224-610373   Fax: + 224-610960

Sierra Leone Work Oxen Programme
(Attn Abu Bakar BANGURA and Bai KANU)
Private Mail Bag 766, Freetown, SIERRA LEONE
Tel: + 232-22-242167   Fax: + 232-22-242128

South Africa Network on Animal Traction (SANAT)
(Attn: Bruce JOUBERT)
Faculty of Agriculture, University of Fort Hare
Private Bag X1314, Alice, 5700, SOUTH AFRICA
Tel: + 27-4060-22085, 22125, 22232
Fax: + 27-4065-31730
E-mail: SANAT@ufhcc.ufh.ac.za

Tanzania Association for Draught Animal Power (TADAP)
(Attn Dr Nuhu HATIBU)
Department of Agricultural Engineering, Sokoine
University of Agriculture
PO Box 3003, Morogoro, TANZANIA
Tel: + 255-56-3259   Fax: + 255-56-4562
E-mail: dasp@sua.ac.tz

West African Farming Systems Research Network
(Attn: Dr James O OLUKOSI)
National Animal Traction Network, Nigeria
(Attn Dr J O Gefu, NAPRI)
c/o Department Agricultural Economics
Institute for Agricultural Research, Ahmadu Bello
University, PMB 1044, Zaria, NIGERIA

networking for development

101

Zambia Animal Power Programme
(Attn: Martin BWALYA)
Palabana Farm Power and Mechanisation Centre
Private Bag 173, Woodlands, Lusaka, ZAMBIA
Tel: + 260-1-611179   Fax: + 260-1-252824

Other formal networks described in this book

Association for Farming Systems Research and Extension
(AFSRE)
(Being a decentralized network, there are board
members in many countries, including the following
representatives from Africa, Asia and Europe)

Raymond AUERBACH,
Farmer Support Group, PO Box 2349,
Hillcrest 3650, SOUTH AFRICA
Tel: + 27-325-3-4412   Fax: + 27-331-6-8485
E-mail: auerbachr@fsg.unp.ac.za

Dr. Namil RANAWEERA,
Ministry of Agriculture, Lands and Forestry,
Sampathpaya, Battaramulla, SRI LANKA
Tel/ Fax: + 94-1-872096
E-mail: minagr@slt.lk

Prof Dr Werner DOPPLER,
University of Hohenheim, Institute of Agricultural
Economics and Social Sciences (490),
70593 Stuttgart, GERMANY
Tel: + 49-711-459-2514   Fax: + 49-711-459-3812
E-mail: doppler@uni-hohenheim.de

Building Advisory Services and Information Network
(BASIN)
(Attn: Otto RUSKULIS)
ITDG, Myson House, Railway Terrace, Rugby
CV21 3HT, UK
Tel: + 44-1788-560631   Fax: + 44-1788-540270
E-mail itdg@itdg.org.uk

Duryog Nivaran
  (Attn: Madhavi ARIYABANDU)
  c/o ITDG, 5 Lionel Edirisinghe Mawatha,
  Kirulapone, Colombo 5, SRI LANKA
  Tel: + 94-1-852149   Fax: + 94-1-856188
  E-mail: dnnet@itdg.lanka.net
  URL: http://www.adpc.ait.th/duryog

Innovations et Réseaux pour le Developpement (IRED)
  3 rue de Varembé, Case 116, 1211 Geneva 20,
  SWITZERLAND
  Tel: + 41-22-734-1716   Fax: + 41-22-740-0011
  E-mail: ired@worldcom.ch

International Federation of Organic Agriculture Movements
  (IFOAM)
  c/o Ökozentrum Imsbach, D-66636 Tholey-Theley,
  GERMANY
  Tel: +49-6853-5190   Fax: +49-6853-30110
  E-mail: ifoam-secretary@oln.comlink.apc.org
  URL: http://ecoweb.dk/ifoam

MandE
  (Attn: Rick DAVIES)
  82 Bishops Road, Trumpington, Cambridge
  CB2 2NH, UK
  Tel/Fax: + 44-1223-841367
  E-mail: rick@shimbir.demon.co.uk
  URL: http://www.shimbir.demon.co.uk

Shelter Forum
  (Attn: Toni SITTONI or Elijah AGEVI)
  c/o ITDG, Box 39493, Nairobi, KENYA
  Tel: +254-2-446243/ 442108
  Fax: +254-2-445166
  E-mail: toni@itdg.or.ke
      elijah@itkenya.comsol.sprint.com

**networking for
development**